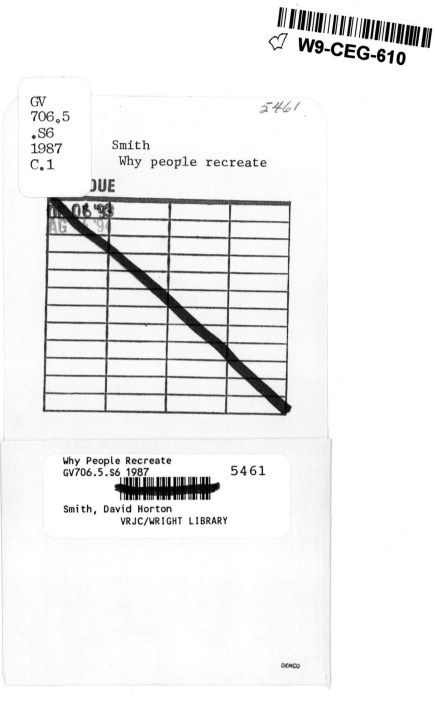

# WHY PEOPLE RECREATE

# WHY PEOPLE RECREATE

## An Overview of Research

**David H. Smith, PhD**
Boston College

**Nancy Theberge, PhD**
University of Waterloo

**Life Enhancement Publications**
Champaign, Illinois

Photographs taken from the following sources:
p. 1, Reprinted, by permission, from Chris Pepper Shipman, *I'll Meet You at the Finish!*, p. 20, in press, Life Enhancement Publications;
p. 9, Reprinted courtesy of The Champaign-Urbana (IL) News-Gazette;
p. 25, Reprinted, by permission, from Chris Pepper Shipman, *I'll Meet You at the Finish!*, p. 51, in press, Life Enhancement Publications;
p. 55, Reprinted, by permission, from Cinda Kochen and Janet McCabe, *The Baby Swim Book*, p. 95, 1986, Leisure Press;
p. 73, Reprinted courtesy of the Champaign (IL) Park District;
p. 83, Reprinted courtesy of The Champaign-Urbana (IL) News-Gazette;
p. 93, Reprinted, by permission, from Keith Rogers. Photo by Thomas Ovalle;
p. 111, Reprinted courtesy of Parcourse Ltd., P.O. Box 99589, San Francisco, CA 94109;
p. 119, Reprinted, by permission, from Chris Pepper Shipman, *I'll Meet You at the Finish!*, p. 121, in press, Life Enhancement Publications.

Library of Congress Cataloging-in-Publication Data

Smith, David Horton.
  Why people recreate.

  Bibliography: p.
  1. Leisure—Social aspects.    2. Outdoor recreation—
Social aspects.    3. Recreational surveys.    I. Theberge,
Nancy.    II. Title.
GV706.5.S6     1987        790'.01'35          82-83933
ISBN 0-87322-902-9

Developmental Editor: Patricia Sammann
Production Director: Ernie Noa
Copy Editor: Ann Morris Bruehler
Typesetter: Sandra Meier
Text Layout: Denise Peters
Cover Design and Layout: Jack Davis
Cover Illustration: Keith Blomberg

ISBN: 0-87322-902-9

Printed in the United States of America

10  9  8  7  6  5  4  3  2  1

Life Enhancement Publications
Box 5076   Champaign, IL 61820

# Contents

# Preface

The aim of this volume is to review the literature on sport and recreation, particularly outdoor recreation, in order to better answer the question "Why do people participate in these activities?" The scope of the research literature reviewed is comprehensive, although it is also selective, so that not every known study on a given topic is cited. Following an introductory chapter that takes up definitional issues, the bulk of the volume considers a wide variety of types of variables that have been found to affect individual participation in recreation and sport. These categories are drawn from the first author's analytical model for the explanation of socioculturally valued discretionary time participation. This Interdisciplinary Sequential Specificity Time Allocation Lifespan (ISSTAL) Model and the categories of variables it contains are interdisciplinary in nature and include some historical as well as sociological and psychological factors. The literature review confirms generally the validity of the ISSTAL Model. Furthermore, it confirms a more specified variant of the model called the General Activity Model (see Smith & Macaulay, 1980). Finally, the concluding chapter contains both a theoretical and methodological critique of the research literature reviewed.

This volume will be a useful introduction to the study of recreation and sport participation for students in sociology, psychology, kinesiology, physical education, and leisure studies, whether used as a basic text or auxiliary reading. However, the volume will also be useful to scholars and researchers in the field of sport and recreation in various ways. It will allow specialists in a particular area of individual participation to see how that area fits into the larger context of relevant research. It will give scholars *not* directly concerned with individual participation an analytical overview of this field. And it will give researchers in the field a clear idea of where future research is most needed, so that they can spend their research time most productively and fruitfully. Finally, for those scholars concerned with the study of leisure or discretionary time most broadly, this volume represents a concrete application of two theoretical models of broad scope, showing that these models can usefully make sense in a cumulative manner of a very large body of research that otherwise seems to lack theoretical integration.

We are indebted to a number of people for their help in typing or photocopying portions of this volume, particularly to Lorraine Bone and Sara White. We also would like to thank the staff of SIRLS at The University of Waterloo for help in retrieving many of the sources cited in this volume.

David Horton Smith
Nancy Theberge

# CHAPTER ONE

# *Introduction*

The study of leisure behavior has grown rapidly in the past decade or so, both in North America and elsewhere. Some sense of the growth involved can be obtained by examining such sources as Meyersohn (1969), van der Smissen and Joyce (1970), Crandall, Altengarten, Nolan, and Dixon (1977), Kelly (1982), a recent issue of the journal *Social Forces* (1981, December) devoted to the sociology of leisure, and the *International Directory of Leisure Information Resource Centres* (Knoop & Kenyon, 1980). The latter volume describes the services and holdings of 47 resource centers located in 19 countries across the world.

Much of the focus of the study of leisure has been on sport and various forms of outdoor recreation, with less attention to participation in indoor table games or hobbies, cultural events and activities (e.g., attending the theater or museums), and adult educational activities for credit, enjoyment, or self-improvement. For this reason, the principal focus here will be on participation in sport and recreation, particularly outdoor recreation. This focus will do some violence to the perspectives of most specialists in the study of leisure, for they generally prefer a much broader definition of leisure. But we are not proposing to review all leisure studies in this volume. Rather, we shall selectively review those leisure studies dealing with sport and recreational participation by individuals.

According to Kaplan (1960), in a classic definition, "the essential elements of leisure . . . are (a) an antithesis to 'work' as an economic function, (b) a pleasant expectation and recollection, (c) a minimum of involuntary social-role obligations, (d) a psychological perception of freedom, (e) a close relation to values of the culture, (f) the inclusion of an entire range from inconsequence and insignificance to weightiness and importance, and (g) often, but not necessarily, an activity characterized by the element of play" (p. 22). Another widely cited definition is that of Dumazedier (1967): "Leisure is activity—apart from the obligations of work, family, and society—to which the individual turns at will, for either relaxation, diversion, or broadening his knowledge and his spontaneous social participation, the free exercise of his creative capacity" (p. 16). And after reviewing various definitions, Neulinger (1974) suggests the following as a primary definition of leisure: "Freedom or, to be more specific, *perceived freedom*. By this we mean a state in which the person feels that what he is doing, he is doing by choice and because he wants to do it" (p. 15). The latter definition permits leisure to overlap with what is paid work if one is gaining sufficient intrinsic satisfaction from it. Still another more recent definitional review is provided by Kelly (1982), who discusses definitions of leisure in terms of time, activity, experience, and meaning, and settles upon a preferred definition of leisure as "activity chosen primarily for its own sake. The dimensions of freedom and intrinsic satisfaction are seen as the central defining elements" (p. 31). However it is defined, there is general agreement that leisure is an increasingly important part of human life in industrial and especially postindustrial society (see Dumazedier, 1967; Kaplan & Bosserman, 1971).

But our concern here is with a narrower realm of sport and recreational types of leisure activity. Scholars have given a good deal of attention to the definition of sport, games, and recreation as special aspects of leisure activity. To understand any of these concepts fully, one must go back to the work of Huizinga (1949), who provided the classic treatment of the nature of play and the quality of an activity's being playful. As further interpreted by Caillois (1955), play may be defined as individual activity that is free (meaning voluntary and uncoerced), separate (in the sense of being spatially and temporally limited), uncertain of outcome, unproductive of material goods, governed by rules (whether formally or informally agreed upon), and possessing a kind of "make-believe" quality (involving pretense and standing apart from ordinary everyday life in some sense). With this as background, Loy (1968) defines a *game* "as any form of playful competition whose outcome is determined by physical skill, strategy or chance employed singly or in combination" (p. 1). (See also Roberts, Arth, & Bush, 1959.) As such, games are a subclass of play, but not a wholly contained subclass, for there can be professional games with paid participants doing their jobs for money, not for fun. Finally, Loy (1968) defines sport in two different but related ways: One way is "to define *a sport* as any highly organized game requiring physical prowess" (p. 2). His second and preferred way is "to define *a sport* as an institutionalized game demanding the demonstration of physical prowess" (p. 2). The latter puts more emphasis on the fact that a sport is a sociocultural pattern, while a game can be seen as either a pattern or an occurrence.

In terms of the foregoing definitions, this book will be concerned with, in part, those games requiring physical prowess (sport) but not with nonphysical games (e.g., board games, card games, etc.). We omit consideration of the latter because there has been so little research there. We shall also be concerned with those kinds of relatively unorganized play that require physical exertion, which we shall term "recreation" or "recreational activity" (indoor or outdoor). Recreation, as Nash (1962) and many others have pointed out, is not merely leisure or free time and not merely "doing nothing" or merely looking on at some amusement or entertainment. Recreation is a physical outlet for playfulness, creativity, and self-expression. In Kelly's (1982) formulation, recreation is restorative, providing refreshment or re-creation, not only for work but for other social (familial, political, etc.) activities.

In the view of Edwards (1973), recreation and sport or athletics are almost mutually exclusive in their essential characteristics, with games overlapping these two concepts in part. That is, he sees some recreation as involving games and some sport and athletics as involving games, but not all of either recreation or sport and athletics is captured by the term "games." Loy (1968) sees sport and athletics as necessarily involving physical exertion, as having an imperative formal hierarchical arrangement of roles and positions and a formal history and recognized records and traditions, and as necessarily involving preparation for participation in the activity. All these characteristics differentiate sport and athletics from other kinds of games that do not have these qualities. Recreation may be distinguished from sport and athletics as an activity *not* requiring the four characteristics just mentioned, as well as by not necessarily involving competition, by being more individually oriented and subject to the starting-and-stopping wishes of the individual, by being more spontaneous and less constrained by rules as a necessity, and by having most of the elements of play described earlier. We would differ with Edwards in viewing recreation, as the concept is used here, as *necessarily* involving physical exertion, where he does not. Our approach is consistent with the broad definition of sport discussed by Claeys (1985), which "refers not only to the commonly recognized sports but also to all possible forms of physical movement in the recreational sphere that are oriented to stimulating and maintaining fitness and physical condition" (p. 234).

Having given some brief attention to connotative definitions of sport and recreation, perhaps it would be useful to give some denotative definitions of these two key terms. Denotative definitions simply indicate or list the types of things to which a concept refers. For instance, common examples of sport would be baseball, handball, soccer, football, basketball, wrestling, track and field, badminton, table tennis, tennis, boxing, swimming, diving, and a great variety of other activities when done in some sort of competitive and formal or quasi-structured circumstances. When these activities are done very informally, noncompetitively (which is virtually impossible for many of the foregoing), or individually, such activities may be viewed as recreation. In addition to swimming and diving noted above, some common examples of recreational activities (when done noncompetitively) are camping, fishing, hunting, backpacking, hiking, walking, jogging, bicycling, golfing, boating (rowing, canoeing), skiing, waterskiing, skydiving, exercising, gardening, horseback riding, sailing, surfing, skin diving or scuba diving, ice-skating, and so on. Extensive lists of sport and recreational activities can be found in Bishop, Jeanrenaud, and Lawson (1975), Chapin (1974), Kelly (1973), McKechnie (1974), Nielson and Catton (1971), and Witt (1971).

It is also important to make clear that our concern here is with individual discretionary time and informal voluntary social participation. Excluded from consideration are all forms of professional sport and those forms of so-called amateur sport (such as Olympic level) that require extensive commitment and investments of time and money and are, in effect, "professional." (For a discussion of the imprecision in the use of the terms *amateur* and *professional* and a reconceptualization of the distinction between the two, see Stebbins, 1979.)

Before going into the detailed review of why individuals participate in sport and recreational activities, it is worthwhile to take a quick look at some worthy overviews of research on recreation and sport. Burdge and Field (1972) have suggested that there are six main perspectives used in the study of outdoor recreation: (a) a social aggregate-level perspective that relates individual recreational activity to social background variables of the usual sort and, more recently, to some "demand" variables; (b) social-psychological approaches that attempt to relate attitudes and values to choice of recreational activities (without, however, consideration of underlying motives and needs); (c) a social-organizational approach that focuses on how recreational activity is affected by the group or organizational contexts in which it takes place and which may influence it; (d) an activity-attributes approach of "widespread interest, but little research" that maintains "that each recreation activity has a type of person which it attracts to the general exclusion of other activities" (pp. 64-65); (e) community and regional analyses that examine the effect of the larger community/territorial context on recreational behavior; and (f) a social ecology approach, little used so far, that attempts to "include the interdependent relationships of population, social organization, environment, and technology" (pp. 64-65) (an attempt to be holistic in the study of recreational participation). Time sampling methods have been suggested as useful for the study of leisure behavior (Peirce, 1975), as have time budget methods, of course (Foote, 1961), cross-cultural comparative methods (Allardt, 1967), participant observation (Campbell, 1970) and phenomenological approaches (Dawson, 1984), telephone interviews (Field, 1973), and historical and philosophical methods (Beamish, 1981; Critcher, 1982; Ingham, 1979). A general overview of research methods that have been employed in the sociology of sport is contained in Loy and Segrave (1974). (See also Whitson, 1978.)

Brown, Dyer, and Whaley (1975) summarize the major criticisms leveled against recreation research as follows:

1. It has not been addressed to solving real problems. It is important to have an answer when someone says, "So what?"
2. It has been reductionist in dealing with only small segments of comprehensive problems and with its fragmentation into discipline-specific, non-integrative projects.
3. The modeling done in recreation has dealt solely with prediction and has not been addressed to understanding.
4. It has not dealt with the recreation phenomenon in the broader context of man's total life style.
5. There has been no development of a theoretical orientation to guide it.
6. It has often been undertaken by researchers poorly prepared to deal with the problems of a multi-disciplinary phenomenon. (p. 17)*

Several of these points are echoed in the major critiques of research in the sociology of sport. McPherson (1978b), for example, has argued that "the sociology of sport is in chaos because the existing body of

---

*From "Recreation Research—So What?" by P.J. Brown, A. Dyer, and R.S. Whaley, 1975, *Journal of Leisure Research,* 5, p. 17. Copyright 1975 by ARPA. Reprinted by permission.

knowledge is comprised of many unrelated descriptive facts and little cumulative explanatory knowledge" (p. 74). In a companion piece, Gruneau (1978) has cited the growing dissatisfaction in the field with "vague theoretical debates" and "the static descriptive analyses and isolated 'social facts' that define the bulk of research in the subdiscipline" (p. 80). In short, it appears that work in the sociology of recreation and sport suffers from problems similar to those attributed to social behavioral science research in the first chapter of Smith and Macaulay (1980).

As a response to those problems, Smith and Macaulay (1980) developed a static theoretical model called the ISSTAL Model. ISSTAL is an acronym for Interdisciplinary Sequential Specificity Time Allocation Lifespan. The aim of the model is to reform social science research on discretionary time behavior, including leisure, volunteering, mass media use, amateur politics, religion, and the like. Central to the model is the notion of using a wide range of explanatory variables when studying any discretionary time activity. This range includes external contextual factors, social background and social role variables, personality traits and intellectual capacities, attitudinal dispositions (values, attitudes, expectations, and intentions), retained information (images, beliefs, knowledge, and plans), and situational variables (immediate awareness and definition of the situation). The interdisciplinary nature of these variables is emphasized, and they are to be seen as affecting behavior in the order just listed in terms of increasing specificity. The present volume follows that ordering in chapters reviewing what is known about explaining and predicting outdoor recreation and sport participation.

The General Activity Model is a variant of the ISSTAL Model that makes additional assumptions and predictions. It holds that human beings adapt their bodies and characters to the sociocultural system (SCS) in which they are embedded. As part of this adaptation, "discretionary social participation activities of all kinds tend to fall into cumulative patterns . . . such that socioculturally encouraged (valued, acceptable) discretionary activity exhibits significant positive covariation or correlation across types of activity, across subtypes of activity, and through time for both types and subtypes of activity" (Smith & Macaulay, 1980, p. 462). This means that in the general population there are positive correlations among various activities within certain areas, such as political activity or positively evaluated recreational activity. It also means that positively evaluated types of discretionary activity correlate significantly with activities in other areas, for example political activities with recreational activities with print media exposure and so on.

On the whole, people's choices of activities for their discretionary time are adaptations to their sociocultural system. However, those in more dominant status positions (especially a higher social class) tend to fit the General Activity Pattern of intercorrelated, higher amounts of discretionary activity. Those higher in general activity also tend to be higher in terms of active-effective character, with personality characteristics and attitudes that favor active participation. For example, the traits of extraversion and self-confidence tend to be positively associated with the General Activity Pattern, as are positive general and specific attitudes toward various kinds of activity and toward the community in general. These elements of the General Activity Model are broadly confirmed by the studies reviewed in the present volume.

# CHAPTER TWO

# *Social and Historical Context Variables*

There are four types of social and historical context factors that might influence individual sport and recreational participation. They are human population factors, biophysical environmental variables, cultural variables, and social structure variables. We will consider each in turn.

## *Human Population Factors*

DeGrazia (1962) has spoken of the difference that the first type, human population factors such as average diet, use of alcoholic or other drinks and drugs, general health, age-sex-race composition, and population density, might make in leisure behavior of individuals in particular societies at particular times. Yet, to our knowledge, there have been no systematic empirical studies on the effects of such factors over time in a given society or across societies at a given time. This is a clear gap in the literature on the determinants of individual sport and recreation participation.

# Biophysical Environmental Variables

For the second type of context factor, biophysical environmental variables, the situation is a bit better but still very poor in terms of the quantity and quality of research available regarding effects on sport and recreational participation or other leisure activities. There are only a few pieces of research worth noting here. Roberts et al. (1959), for instance, performed a study of games of physical skill, strategy, and chance using data on preliterate tribal societies from the Human Relations Area Files. Selecting about 100 tribes from all over the world and with wide cultural variability, they sought detailed information on the games played in each society. The topic of games was well covered in the ethnographic descriptions of about 50 tribes. Most tribes had *some* kind of games; only 5 did not. Most widespread were games of physical skill, followed by games of strategy and chance in about equal numbers but much less widespread. Of principal interest here is the fact that the number of games of physical skill reported in a society was significantly higher when the society was located more than 20° north or south of the equator. This suggests that mean temperature, humidity, or aspects of diet related to latitude on the earth may have something to do with sport and recreational participation as a contextual variable.

There are only a few other studies that deal with climatic effects on participation. Michelson (1971) studied the social participation of 173 married women with children living in metropolitan Toronto, with interviews in late February and reinterviews in late June. Completed interviews for both data points were obtained on 130 women, all relatively homogeneous in socioeconomic status and family composition. Sport participation frequencies showed a marked increase from winter to summer, with a net shift of 28% toward higher participation in June among those participating in February. The shift was also positive for church or synagogue attendance but was generally negative for such leisure activities as arts and crafts, adult education courses, attending meetings, and telephoning. Other activities examined showed little seasonal change, but the list was not very extensive (18 activities, many of them related to work or home and social obligations). Another analysis of the effects of seasonality was performed by Sutton-Smith (1953), who examined the effects of climatic changes upon the games that New Zealand children played. The results of his investigation among children aged 7 to 12 showed little seasonal effect in that few games were played in specific seasons.

A more important study, based on the Szalai, Converse, Feldheim, Scheuch, and Stone (1972) data, is by Converse (1972). Using time budget data from close to 30,000 people in 12 different nations, Converse found clear evidence of a "North-South" dimension in national variations in average patterns. Careful examination of particular types of activities accounting for the North-South dimension makes it clear that a climatic factor is responsible, with people in warmer climates spending more time sleeping, resting, and in outdoor activities, including recreation and sport. In the colder countries more time is spent on mass media consumption, religion, organizations, shopping, and personal care. These data support the conclusion drawn from the more limited Michelson data that participation in sport and recreation is likely to be greater in warmer countries and in the warmer seasons of the year. But the earlier study by Roberts et al. (1959) suggests that getting too close to the equator can have the reverse effect. In the Converse study, of the 12 countries studied, only Peru was at all close to the equator. Future research will probably reveal a curvilinear relationship such that sport and recreation participation will be greatest in temperate climates and seasons (not too hot, too cold, too stormy, etc.) and least in climates and seasons with extremes of average temperature or usually characterized by poor weather conditions. Robinson (1977) indicates, for instance, that outdoor leisure activities are less frequent in the U.S. in poor weather. However, Godin and Matz (1976) find no such effect for long-distance wilderness hikers, especially if they have driven far to the hiking trail.

One other important source of data on climatic and seasonal effects on sport and recreation participation is a study by Cicchetti (1972). He looked at seasonal participation rates for 21 specific sport and recreational activities as indicated by a large U.S. national sample survey performed in the early 1960s. As might be expected, many of the results are activity specific, with swimming being a summer sport, hunting a fall and winter activity, and sports such as ice-skating, sledding, and snow skiing being mainly confined to winter. In general, the results indicate that the summer is the season when participation rates in active outdoor sport and recreation are highest, whether measured in terms of percentage participating or number of days on which individuals have engaged in the activity.

Another major biophysical environmental variable that has received some attention is rural-urban residence and particularly the related variable of availability of relevant sport and recreational facilities. Rural-versus-urban residence is an ambiguous proxy variable for many possible contextual variables. The need for more careful study of such differences is well described by Hendee (1969). After noting that Nielson (1969) found nearly 90 references in 20 articles to hypothetical urban-rural differences in outdoor recreation, Hendee (1969) reports that results of a study by the national Outdoor Recreation Resource

Review Commission (ORRRC) (1962a) show little rural-urban difference in participation once the usual social background factors are held
constant. On the surface, urbanites appear to be overrepresented in
most kinds of outdoor recreation and sport in the U.S. (Hendee, 1969;
McKnelly, 1973), though not in the Netherlands (Wippler, 1968). Careful analysis, however, shows that most of this variation stems from
the social background factors of income, education, and occupation
rather than location.

Another important factor involved in rural-urban differences is
"opportunity structure" or availability of facilities or locations for sport
and recreation. Hauser (1962) draws two related conclusions in this
regard after his analysis of the ORRRC data:

> The first is that increasing urbanization may diminish the importance
> of outdoor recreation activity, in general, as well as that of a number
> of present specific forms of outdoor recreations activity. The data sug-
> gest that with increased urbanization those forms of outdoor recre-
> ation which are, on the whole, restricted to the nonurban environment
> and which require a great deal of physical vigor and relative dis-
> comfort, become increasingly unimportant as forms of leisure-time
> activity. . . . The second conclusion is that those forms of outdoor
> recreation activity which are associated with the urban environment
> or which may be as readily pursued within or near it as in nonurban
> areas are already much more important than the above activities and
> may become increasingly important as measured by demand during
> the remainder of this century. These include the 5 most popular of
> the 20 specific forms of outdoor recreation activity for whicn data were
> collected in the National Recreational Survey, namely: picnics (53 per-
> cent), driving for pleasure (52 percent), swimming (45 percent), sight-
> seeing (42 percent), walking for pleasure (33 percent). They also
> include (with the possible exception of fishing) all of the other specific
> outdoor activities which involve the participation of at least 20 per-
> cent of the population; playing outdoor games or sports (30 percent),
> fishing (29 percent), attending outdoor sports events (24 percent), boat-
> ing other than canoeing or sailing (22 percent). (p. 51)

Other studies, with more limited and specialized samples, support similar conclusions regarding the importance of opportunity factors as determinants of individual sport and recreation participation.
Before turning to such studies, however, it is interesting to note that
other analyses of the ORRRC data supported the Hauser conclusions
regarding the importance of facilities and opportunity structure. For
instance, Cicchetti (1972) reviews several analyses that added variables
representing the relative availability (quantity) and quality of recreational facilities in the county and state of residence of each respon-
dent. When standard socioeconomic status (SES) background variables
were controlled in multivariate analyses, the opportunity structure variables explained significant amounts of variance in level of individual

participation for various activities. However, opportunity structure variables did not increase the explained variance in basic participation rates (whether or not an individual participates in a given activity at all). Cicchetti (1972) concluded that "the supply or facility variables proved to be a more important set of constraints in determining the intensity or number of days of participation than in determining the probability of participation and were generally positively related in quantity and quality to participation patterns" (p. 104).

There are some studies with more limited samples that also show the importance of the opportunity structure. Meldrum (1971) found that participation in climbing, canoeing, caving, and skiing was related to the opportunities for such activities in four European countries. Treble and Neil (1972) found that women's participation in sport was related to the availability of sport facilities for women in urban areas, which in turn was related to cultural attitudes toward the social role of women. Leigh (1971) found readily available sport and recreational facilities to be crucial to the leisure time activities. Kiviaho (1973) examined the effect of level of industrialization in Finnish communes upon membership in sport clubs. Level of industrialization was measured by the proportion of all gainfully employed who worked in industrial (manufacturing and service) occupations. He found a positive but non-linear relationship between industrialization and club membership in moderately industrialized communities. In order to examine the possible confounding effects of sex, age, and education, Kiviaho reexamined the zero order relationship controlling for these variables. The controlling procedure did not significantly alter the results, and the original association remained.

## Cultural Variables

Turning to cultural variables, the third type of context factor that may affect sport and recreation participation, we find more relevant research than for human population and biophysical factors, though systematic comparative studies are very rare, and impressionistic material is usual. For instance, one finds in anthologies on the sociology of sport sections that deal with "sport and culture" or "sport and society." These describe how different specific nations view particular sport or recreational activities (see Loy & Kenyon, 1969; Smith, Parker, & Smith, 1973; Talamini & Page, 1973), sometimes with reference to quantitative empirical studies (see Anderson, Bo-Jensen, El Kaer-Hansen, & Sonne, 1969). Other works on sport and national communities include Lever (1983) on Brazilian soccer and Riordan (1977,

1980) on sport in the Soviet Union. Along these lines, Guttmann (1978) discusses the attraction of nations to particular sports, with a case analysis of baseball and football in the United States.

There are also a number of high quality historical studies of the rise of sport and recreation of various types in the United States and elsewhere (Betts, 1974; Gerber, 1974; Gruneau, 1983; Hardy, 1982; Henderson, 1953; Manchester, 1968; McIntosh, Dixon, Munrow, & Willetts, 1957; Metcalfe, 1978; Rader, 1983; Steiner, 1970; Weaver, 1968). Some of these, such as Betts' *America's Sporting Heritage: 1850-1900* (see also Betts, 1954), are exceedingly well done and show the interconnections of cultural and social structural variables as determinants of sport and recreational participation. As part of his analysis Betts shows how a single kind of cultural change, the introduction of new technology, affected the whole range of sport and recreation in America over a 50-year period. The effect of transportation, communication, lighting, electrification, cameras, sport equipment, and related inventions on sport activity during this period was revolutionary for amateur as well as professional sport and recreation. Another example of excellent historical scholarship is Mandell's *Sport: A Cultural History* (1984). This work provides a detailed account and analysis of sport in classical Greece, early industrial England, and the United States. In addition to general histories of sport and recreation, there are many histories of specific kinds of sport or recreation (Andreano, 1965; Dunning & Sheard, 1979; Goodspeed, 1939; Hervey, 1944; Miermans, 1955). More broadly, Sutton-Smith and Rosenberg (1961) have shown long-term cultural changes in children's game choices.

All of these studies point up the important fact that sport and recreation participation by individuals is strongly historically and culturally conditioned. The same is true to a lesser extent for various forms of outdoor recreation. Some recreation is so nearly universal (swimming, hunting, and fishing) that historical and cultural factors tend to be mainly important in timing and location of the activity. Furthermore, there are cultural variations not only in the existence of a sport (as an institutionalized cultural pattern) in a society, but also in the prestige value of a given sport, which has a major effect on participation by various classes of individuals.

An excellent example of the latter kind of effect can be found in a study by Rogers (1974) dealing with normative aspects of leisure time behavior in the Soviet Union. On the basis of secondary analysis of research reports by Soviet sociologists, she concluded that there is a prestige hierarchy of sport and recreational pursuits in that country. Most favored are cultural and educational activities (such as reading, attending the theater, concerts, literature readings, exhibits, or museums), sport, and art activities. Less favored are mass media exposure activities (radio listening, television viewing, and movie attendance). Actual participation rates do not parallel such cultural preferences perfectly (for example, television viewing is high while its prestige is low), but the correspondence is rather good. Rogers notes that various studies lead to the conclusion "that there is indeed much more agreement among adults in the Soviet Union on what one ought to do with one's leisure time, than there is agreement in patterns of actual leisure time behavior. The most highly educated live up most closely to the norms. . . . The print media have the highest prestige among the mass media. . . . Sports and amateur art activities also fall into this category [of desirable things to do], as do probably hobbies" (p. 378).

Several studies of other nations yield similar conclusions regarding variations in the prestige and acceptability of different sport and recreational activities. For instance, Sutton-Smith, Roberts, and Kozelka (1963), using several American surveys, have shown variation by SES and sex in leisure activity, with games of strategy "associated with women and higher status, games of chance with women and lower status, and games of physical skill with men and higher status" (p. 21). These results are interpreted in terms of differential child-rearing practices that vary by sex and SES. An extension of this work among Israeli children by Eifermann (1971), however, produced only partial confirmation of the earlier results. The most striking contrasts were that there was no preference for games of chance among females and members of low-status groups, and games of strategy were preferred by high-status children but not by females. Luschen (1969) found class variations in popularity and participation levels for different sport and recreational activities in West Germany. Tennis, field hockey, and skiing were high-status sports, while table tennis, badminton, canoeing, and apparatus gymnastics were low-status sports, with field athletics and association football lowest of all. Iso-Ahola (1975) compared the leisure time preferences of Finnish and American youth. Time budget data were collected from secondary school students in cities in the two nations. The results showed that American students had more active leisure time and were more involved in sport and recreational activities than the Finnish students. Some differences were attributed to a decline in the popularity of sport among the Finnish youth over the past decade (see Aalto, 1971; Allardt et al., 1958). Of these several studies, Luschen's is particularly important in suggesting that the newer the sport, the higher the social prestige of the sport. Cost of involvement is another factor that may well affect prestige levels of sports (the higher the cost, the higher the prestige) because such constraints will tend to limit participation and make for a kind of exclusivity that is often found with higher status activities.

Of course, the theoretical premise that sport participation is related to social class is not new in sociology. Veblen (1899), in his *Theory of the Leisure Class,* suggested that sport and recreational activities were characteristic activities primarily of the leisure class. There is some debate regarding the degree to which social barriers to involvement have dissolved and sport has become a mass phenomenon. Evidence of both the widening base of involvement over the past century and the persistence of strata differences is available for many countries. For example, in his historical chronicle of American sport, Betts (1974) argues that sport developed along class lines from 1850-1900, whereas the first half of the 20th century saw a broadening to more mass involvement. Riesman and Denney (1954) have shown, in line with both Luschen (1969) and Veblen (1899), that football in the United States began as an upper-class pastime of students at the high-prestige colleges of Yale and Harvard, later spreading (with changes) to other colleges of lower prestige. (See also the 1958 volume by Larrabee & Meyersohn on "mass leisure.") Burdge (1969), however, has shown the continuing association between social status and participation in a variety of recreational activities in the United States. Metcalfe's (1976, 1978) studies of the organization of Canadian amateur sport in the last half of the 20th century document that growth occurred mainly among the expanding middle class. More recent Canadian data analyzed by Curtis and Milton (1976) and the Canada Fitness Survey (1983) demonstrate a continuing association between sport participation and social class. Other examples of at least partial democratization include Dunning and Sheard's (1979) analysis of the diffusion of British football from the elite public schools in England to the broader society and the study by Anderson et al. (1969) in Denmark showing a generally rising percentage of persons participating in sport over the past decades. Part of this general increase in sport participation comes not only from the diffusion of sport among the middle and lower strata of society but also from the increasing participation of girls and women in sport as gender role norms have changed (see, for instance, Hall & Richardson, 1982). Comparing U.S. time budget data from 1934 with 1965-1966 data, Robinson (1969) shows that average daily sport participation of adult women, whether housewives or employed, has increased markedly over the 3 decades involved. Although the samples are not fully comparable, the high-status bias of the earlier data suggests that the actual increase in female sport participation is likely to have been greater than the two- to tenfold increases shown for various sports.

There are still other explanations for long-term cultural changes in sport participation, particularly in the U.S. and other modern nations. The key factor seems to be the relative importance of the cultural value of achievement. Let us begin by noting that McClelland (1961) found that among preliterate societies those relatively higher in need for achievement as a cultural value (as reflected in folktales) tended to have children who played more competitive and individualistic games (or sports, by our definition). Luschen (1964) pointed out the striking relationship between Protestantism and high individual performance in sport, arguing that religion is here only an intermediate variable, one that ultimately reflects achievement as a cultural value, the true independent variable of importance in comparing nations. Inkeles and Smith (1974) have further shown that with increasing social structural modernization, there tends to come increasing average individual concern for efficacy, aspiration, and achievement, which are presumably also incorporated into the cultural value systems of modern industrial societies (see Williams, 1970). However, when the transition from industrial to postindustrial society (with more focus on tertiary or service industries than upon manufacturing) is made, there may come an additional push toward sport and recreational participation. Wolfenstein (1958) has described this cultural change in highly industrialized societies as the "emergence of the fun morality." Instead of being taboo, as under the earlier work-and-achievement ethic characteristic of societies in the process of active industrialization (Greenberg, 1958), having fun becomes an obligation in the leisure society (see also Dumazedier, 1967). In the terminology of Dubin (1956), work is no longer a "central life interest" of the average worker in society. This is reflected in a general trend toward earlier retirement by employed workers and the growth of a national ethos of leisure in the United States, as well as in other postindustrial societies (Barfield & Morgan, 1969; Lowenthal, 1966). However, there is some ambivalence involved in this change, as Riesman (1958), Burns (1973), and Charlesworth (1964) have pointed out in different ways. Too much may be demanded of leisure by the individual (for instance, instant self-fulfillment or happiness of an enduring sort), and many individuals may be unprepared to take full advantage of the increasing leisure that is made available to them, and indeed sometimes forced upon them, by changing cultural values regarding work and leisure. Today's "workaholic" would have been prized rather than denigrated in earlier stages of industrialization. In the future, people with overabundant energy and achievement drive may become "sportaholics," frenetically competing and participating in numerous sport and recreational activities that are supposed to be "fun."

## Social Structure Variables

The fourth type of social-historical context factor, social structure variables, has been found to have an even clearer impact on sport and recreational participation than cultural variables. One of the most well-studied variables is available discretionary time, as determined both by the occupational structure of society and by the price of free time in terms of opportunity cost (time when one could be working and earning money instead). According to Clawson (1964), the total national time budget from 1900-1950 showed an increase of discretionary or leisure time from 27-34% of the total. By the year 2000 the figure will be 38%. Most of the past and future increase has and will come from increased retirement and vacation leisure. The introduction of the 8-day week (Pearson, 1973) or the 4-day, 40-hour week (Poor, 1970) may be expected to have additional major impacts on the pattern of leisure time activities, although there are few systematic studies we know of that document such changes.

Careful study and documentation have been done in the area of discretionary time available to the individual as a result of social structural changes in the occupational structure, changes stemming largely from the industrial revolution. As Soule (1957) and others have pointed out, economic development and industrialization have made increasing amounts of leisure time available to most people over the past centuries. Leisure time is no longer something enjoyed only by the rich. Cottrell (1961) sees increased productivity and efficient energy use as the chief proximate causes of this change, while Wilensky (1961) documented the decline of the average work week for the period from about 1850-1950. Dumazedier (1967) and others have heralded the coming of the "leisure society." However, still others have challenged this vision (De Grazia, 1962). Perhaps the most compelling presentation of the counterview that the decline in work time has leveled off and that work time may even increase is to be found in an article by Carter (1970). He concludes that "the two basic factors that are tending to increase the amount of work activity are: (1) the change in management philosophy toward increased job enrichment, which will make time spent with the corporation more rewarding for all employees; and (2) the low productivity per man hour in the growing service occupations which will increase the opportunity for extended work-weeks" (p. 65). Further, "the basic factor that is tending to decrease the amount of work activity [in terms of per capita labor force averages] is the increase in female participation in the labor force, especially in the service occupations" (p. 65). We have seen more overtime work and dual-job-holding by paid workers in recent years, and future increases "in non-work activities may only be a realistic expectation for those experiencing 'forced leisure' (e.g., unemployed) or for those who have decided to opt for an alternative life style which does not center around work activities" (p. 65).

Nonetheless, there is general agreement that from the late 1800s to the early middle 1900s, average hours of work per person in the labor force declined markedly, from about 70 hours in 1850 to about 40 hours in recent decades. Major social structural factors in this decline have been the passing of laws restricting work by women and children, the rise in productivity per worker, and a series of laws providing for better working conditions and fringe benefits (Carter, 1970; Zeisel, 1958), particularly more paid vacations and holidays.

These changes in work time and increases in leisure time have been related to increased sport and recreational participation by some authors. For instance, McEvoy (1974) reports on a number of studies of the 4-day, 40-hour week, both in terms of workers' hypothetical preferences and actual experiences with such schedules. The results suggest that this new work schedule tends to increase preferences for and participation in sport and recreation, among other types of leisure activity increases. If this work schedule were widely adopted, it would probably even out demand for recreational resources, thus possibly increasing demand still further by increasing quality of recreational resources. With less crowding day to day, recreation facilities may be more attractive.

With regard to the amount of leisure time, rather than its patterning, some important work has been done by Owen, an economist. In regression analyses of data from the period of 1900-1961 in the United States, Owen (1971) found that "about 25% of the estimated long-term increase in demand for leisure is explained by a decline in market recreation prices" (p. 56). (He held real wage rate constant and hence real income and the relative price of leisure.) The less leisure costs, sport and recreational activity included, the more leisure people will seek, holding real income constant. The demand for leisure time is also related to real income, with higher income demanding more leisure. Owen found that about 75% of the increase in leisure time was associated with increases in the real hourly wage (1971). Owen (1969) also pointed out that "the leveling off of the relative price of recreation since 1929 offers a partial explanation of the observed retardation in the rate of decline over time in hours of work" (p. 151). All of this fits well with the observed spread of sport and recreation from the elite to lower status levels.

Other aspects of work have been suggested as determinants of leisure and of sport and recreational participation in particular. Bose (1957), studying two villages in India, one with a traditional agricultural occupational structure and one where most workers commuted to factory jobs in Calcutta, found marked differences in recreational patterns. In the agricultural village, recreation tended to be collective and seasonal in nature, while in the other village recreation was more constant year-round and more individual in nature.

Similar effects of the occupation structure, particularly with regard to participation of women in the labor force, have been observed in other studies. One effect of the increased employment of women is the reduction of nonpaid activities of all kinds (Balog, 1974). Countering these reductions are the social structural changes in services made in response to increasing needs and ability to pay. These include provision of day-care centers, and opening of more laundries, repair shops, catering facilities, and so on (Stockman, 1974). The effect of occupational structure changes upon time budget patterns has been demonstrated by Converse (1972), using the 12-nation data set gathered by Szalai et al. (1972). Converse found that a principal differentiating factor in time budget patterns from different nations is the proportion of work-related time. Eastern European adults tend to work more hours and to be involved in more work-related activities than Western European or North American adults. Much of this difference reflects the much higher proportion of women who work in Eastern European nations (85% or more) as contrasted with the other countries (30-45%). However, the effect of these differences is much greater on mass media usage and social activities than upon sport and recreation.

Another interesting social structural approach to explaining variations in individual leisure behavior is that taken by Ferge (1972), who also used the Szalai data. She examined the relationship between socioeconomic status and variety in leisure and recreational activity choices. She found that "the social strata show usually significant differences with respect to the variety of activities, better economic means and better cultural preparation leading to a larger range of possible choices. . . . [H]owever, . . . social differentiation does not appear equally sharply in each country or in the case of each variety measure" (p. 222). Also, historical and cultural as well as social structural conditions affect the variety of leisure activities observed. Thus, while social structure has an effect that is similar across countries, there are major exceptions. What precisely accounts for these exceptions is unclear.

Another broad social structural factor that has been suggested to affect leisure participation is the mass media system (see Greendorfer, 1981, 1983). Curran and Tunstall (1973), for instance, argue that in Britain mass media exposure currently totally dominates leisure activity. Robinson and Converse (1972) report similar findings for the United States, though informal conversation and visiting are also major time consumers. The latter go further and suggest that the introduction and growth of television was the single most important factor affecting daily life in the United States since World War II. They note that much of the increase in television viewing had been at the expense of radio listening, but if one goes back further still to prebroadcast-media times, something else must have been filling up this time.

Comparison with data from the early 1930s suggests that sport was among the leisure activities to undergo a major decline over the past several decades, corresponding to the introduction of the broadcast media. (Other types of leisure activities such as reading, attending movies, radio listening, card playing, dancing, and church attendance also suffered a decline.) Generally, the structure of the television and other media industries all have long-term contextual effects on leisure activities. One part of the general trend is a gradual reduction in the amount of time devoted to sport and recreation. However, part of this trend includes the burgeoning growth of commercial sport in the past few decades, which has also doubtless had an important effect on individual sport and recreational participation. As the sport industry has grown and spread into more types of sport and recreation, with everything from professional tennis players to professional skiers nowadays in the United States, there is likely to have been a corresponding drop in direct sport and recreation participation as spectatorship has increased. Unfortunately, there is no adequate data to test this thesis accurately (but see Edwards, 1973).

There are other social structural changes that have caused or promise to cause changes in the nature and degree of sport and recreational participation in industrial and postindustrial societies. The changing role of women in society has been accompanied by some change in the patterns of their involvement in these activities, although the movement toward gender equality in sport is far from complete (see various articles in Oglesby, 1978; also Boutilier & SanGiovanni, 1983; Hall & Richardson, 1982). We have also noted the impact of technological change, which is perhaps more properly treated under the category of cultural variables (Betts, 1974). In addition to the effects of technological change in general upon sport and recreational participation, there are also effects of more specific technological advances in the technology of sport—that is, in the equipment of objects very directly involved in sport and recreation. The effects of such changes have been dealt with by Betts (1954), McIntosh et al. (1957), and Ingham and Singh (1975). There have also been social structural changes in the resource opportunity structure for various kinds of sport as a result of the parks and recreation movement in the United States and elsewhere (see Steiner, 1970, and the 27 study reports of the ORRRC published in the early 1960s by the U.S. Government Printing Office). Not only have there been important increases in the demand for leisure, as noted earlier, but there have also been corresponding increases in the supply of facilities for outdoor recreation and sport. In part these changes can be viewed as aspects of a changing biophysical environment, as we treated them above. However, in part such changes also result from changing social structures—federal, state, and lower level governments becoming more concerned with the provision of such resources and facilities, for instance. An example concerning sport is a discussion of the evolution of federal government policies toward sport in Canada provided in Franks and Macintosh (1984). A related change in resource opportunity structures that may affect sport and outdoor recreation participation is the state of the economy (Wagner & Donohue, 1976). A downturn in the economy reduces outdoor recreation, except among the wealthy, it seems.

Another important social structural variable less frequently studied is the nature of the community or organization in which sport and recreational activities are taking place. One classic study of this sort is Coleman's 1961 study of American high schools. He found different value patterns in the schools that affected the extent to which male students in each school would strive to become athletes in order to win social approval from their peers.

Coleman's study has been followed by a series of partial replications and extensions. Eitzen (1976) conducted a similar investigation in the early 1970s and again found differences among high schools' value climates and a moderate decline in the evaluation of athletics overall. Birrell (1981) extended the analysis to include girls as well as boys in three New England high schools and also found between-school differences as well as a lower valuation of athletics among girls than boys. In the most recent research on this topic that we know of, Thirer and Wright (1985) surveyed high school students in eight U.S. cities. Although they did not report data on between-school differences, they found no major differences on this variable from Eitzen's findings. Additionally, Thirer and Wright found that not only was athletics still the main route to popularity for boys, but it was also still assigned low status for girls. Finally, Friesen (1967) partially replicated Coleman's work among Canadian students from three regions of the country. In a departure from the U.S. findings of Coleman, Eitzen, Birrell, and Thirer and Wright, Friesen found little difference among the schools and a considerably lower valuation of the athletic role than the academic role. None of these more recent studies includes the rather sophisticated analysis of the association between the value climates of schools and students' efforts to achieve athletically that Coleman provides. For this type of analysis Coleman's work remains the sole exemplar, so far as we know.

Investigations of the role of athletics in the school value climate have mainly been conducted in North America. One exception is Engstrom's (1974) study of eighth grade classes in 91 schools in four different Swedish counties. Although Engstrom, unlike Coleman, made no direct measures of values, his results showed very significant school variations in students' self-reported levels of leisure time physical activity for "ordinary" weeks in February and May. Both community and school factors may have been involved. At a still more specific level there are aspects of the particular sport team or club in which an individual is participating, but such factors have received virtually no attention regarding their impact on participation.

## *Future Research*

We may sum up this chapter by saying that all four kinds of contextual variables that are theoretical determinants of individual discretionary behavior have some relevance to understanding sport and recreational participation. However, the quantity and quality of research on these factors is meager. To give a brief overview of possible lines of research that we have only been able to touch on in this section, we can list the characteristics delineated by Kaplan (1960) as distinctive facets of the city versus the rural area that influence leisure. For the urban area, these factors are potentially important:

1. Such facilities as museums, made possible only by very large tax structures.
2. Parks and play areas with excellent facilities and often with expert leadership.
3. Volunteer citizens' organizations whose function it is to work for recreational facilities in the community.
4. Many homes without sufficient play space or facilities within them for children or adults.
5. Large commercial enterprises for recreation that depend on concentrated populations.
6. Many businesses devoted to advertising and selling equipment for leisure use.
7. Transportation facilities to other play spaces, either in the region or across the country.
8. Educational institutions to meet almost every kind of interest.
9. Many kinds of persons with specialized interests who can be called upon for the creation of clubs and hobby groups.
10. Creative centers in the arts, with persons highly skilled in producing works for enjoyment of others and in teaching amateurs.

The rural life, "in its 'pure' form," according to Kaplan, has these potentially important aspects:

1. A generally less hurried pace, so that even with considerable physical labor in farm work there is less psychological and emotional need to relax for therapeutic reasons.

2. A family that is closer together in the sense of awareness of what others are doing and is therefore in less need of leisure as a stabilizing or solidifying factor.
3. With the presence of cars, often the liability to take advantage of city facilities in addition to the ever-present rural patterns and benefits.
4. Longer periods of consecutive free time, as in August on some farms or during the winter months.
5. The development of such organizations as 4-H in which programs contain both educational and recreational activity.
6. The use of the church as a social center for many purposes.
7. Freedom from fads and crazes in leisure.
8. Less class-leisure and therefore less reliance on it as a symbol of distinction.
9. More reliance on local and "natural" leaders, rather than professionals.
10. Fewer choices in entertainment provided by professionals or other persons and therefore more development of resources in the area. (pp. 135-136)*

Many other kinds of contextual factors could be suggested (see the list of Douglass & Crawford, 1964), but Kaplan's lists from 2 decades ago are still reasonably comprehensive ones. It is particularly interesting because, after more than 2 decades, so little has been done to test these hypotheses on sport and recreation.

---

*From *Leisure in America: A Social Inquiry* (pp. 135-136) by M. Kaplan, 1960, New York: Wiley and Sons. Copyright 1960 by M. Kaplan. Reprinted by permission.

# CHAPTER THREE

## *Social Background and Role Characteristics*

As suggested in the second chapter of Smith and Macaulay (1980), there are several major subcategories of social background and role characteristics that may have significant effects on any form of social participation, and within each of these categories there is usually a variety of specific variables to be considered. Because the general accounting scheme for explanatory variables given in that chapter was devised by the senior author of this volume, we have gone to great lengths in this substantive volume on sport and recreational participation to show how the full range of such variables might be significant and, where possible, to seek studies in which each kind has been shown to be significant.

## Health and Physiological Factors

Health and physiological factors have received very little attention in the study of informal or formal social participation. That this generalization should be true also in the study of sport and recreational participation is further testimony to the thesis proposed by Smith (1980) that our understanding of human social participation is seriously hampered by disciplinary boundaries in our choices of explanatory variables. Researchers in the fields of physical education and kinesiology have, of course, done a great deal of research into the physical and physiological factors that make for outstanding performance in competitive athletics and sport. As well, there has been some cross-cultural research into the social correlates and determinants of success in high level (Olympic) amateur sport (Seppanen, 1981). But this research is of little use in understanding informal sport and recreational activities among the general population, especially in noncompetitive sport and recreational activities.

Still, there have been a few studies of general populations or comparisons of athletes with nonathletes that have made use of health and physiological variables to enhance our understanding of why people participate in sport and recreational activities. For instance, Hobart (1975) reports results from a representative sample of 4,300 adults in the province of Alberta, Canada. The data were gathered in lengthy (2-1/2 hour) interviews in 1967. Using self-reported participation in individual or group athletics as the dependent variable, Hobart found that self-reported health was positively related to such participation and self-reported feelings of tiredness after work were negatively related to participation. These relationships held up when the data were examined separately for women and men, but both variables had slightly greater impact among women. Controls for age also failed to change the observed relationships. When separate multiple regression analyses were performed on five sex-by-age groups using a variety of social-background variables and one attitude variable (anomie), self-reported health emerged as an independent contributor to the variance for women of both age groups (most strongly for the middle-aged group). More recently, the Canada Fitness Survey (1983) has shown a positive relationship between activity level and several measures of fitness and self-reported health indicators.

Similar results also emerged from a study by Bultena and Wood (1970) of 322 retired men who migrated from the Midwest to one of four planned retirement communities in Arizona. The respondents, selected randomly from lists of community residents, ranged in age from 51 to 92. They were generally from higher socioeconomic levels and their children tended to be scattered geographically to a greater extent than for nonmigrant aged people. The dependent variable of recreational participation was an index based on respondents' self-report of participation in one or more of a list of 15 activities, including both outdoor recreation and sport as well as indoor recreational activities like dancing, bowling, art, crafts, and card playing. Perceived health status was positively and significantly associated with recreational participation ($r + .15$). The relationship was slightly stronger (partial $r + .17$) when age, income, and education were controlled.

An overview of research on the biological and physical characteristics of sportswomen compiled by Wyrick (1974) shows that in comparison to nonactive women, women engaged in physical activity generally have greater strength and endurance, are taller and heavier, and have a higher muscular component and superior physical support systems. The variety of studies reviewed by Wyrick include samples of women from a range of competitive levels, from Olympic competitors to more recreational participants (e.g., university intramural athletes).

Particularly strong evidence comes from the massive ORRRC national survey of the United States population aged 12 years and over (ORRRC, 1962a). Data from 4,409 cases were analyzed. There, higher self-reported health was found to be consistently and often strongly related to participation in the 17 kinds of outdoor recreation and sport during the summer months of 1960. Results were similar for the other three seasons for both percent participating and days of participation per person measures, and for males and females. No analyses controlling variables other than sex and age were reported. However, the effect of handicap or impairment was explored. As expected, this health-related measure showed similar results to those for the general health measure. Physical impairments or handicaps consistently decrease participation in outdoor recreation and sport. This effect is most pronounced for "limiting impairments" and for the more active forms of recreation, as contrasted with more passive forms (such as walking for pleasure, sightseeing, nature walks, driving for pleasure, camping, or attending an outdoor sport event). There are some reversals of the general trend for the 12- to 17-year-old group of respondents with nonlimiting impairments; this may reflect relatively high levels of activity prescribed as therapy or perhaps some overcompensation. There are also some reversals of the general trend when the participation measure is days per person participation rather than percentage participating, again for those persons with a nonlimiting impairment.

Several small studies have focused on sport and recreation participation as affected by more specific measures of physical fitness, size, abilities, and skills. Dowell (1973) found that college students who had earned a high school athletic letter were more physically fit than a comparison group who had not. Engstrom (1974), in a study of more than 2,000 students randomly selected from eighth-grade classes in four counties in Sweden (chosen to represent large variation in climate in that country), devised a "ponderal index" variable by dividing individuals' height by the cube root of their weight. This body index showed a significant curvilinear relationship with the number of hours spent in sport participation per week for both boys and girls (more strongly for boys). Underweight and overweight students were less likely to engage in sport than were students with average height-weight relationships. Stebbins (1969), studying students in U.S. parochial and public senior high schools, found that nonathletes were smaller in physical size than students who had been high school athletes. He used both height and weight as size measures but did not create a ponderal index. A related finding by Heinila (1964), from a study of 160 Finnish high school classes, indicated that physically weaker students did not participate in various physical activities and sports, particularly the very competitive ones, because they did not want to feel inferior. Among English college students, Kane (1970) found various physical abilities, and particularly muscularity, to be significantly related to sport participation. His study, to which we shall return later, is noteworthy also for seeking and finding relationships between physical abilities of various kinds and personality traits.

Kenyon and McPherson (1973) argue that the development of active sport participation is in part dependent on a "primary sport aptitude," a broad trait that could include all facets of health, fitness, and physical ability. Assuming that this is the case, it is sad that social scientists studying sport and recreational participation for the general population usually neglect to include measures of physical aptitude along with other explanatory variables. The basic role of physical strength and skill as factors in sport and recreational participation should not simply be taken for granted but rather measured adequately and entered appropriately into any multivariate analyses. It is worth recalling here Landtman's (1938) point that in preliterate societies physical strength and skill in games, fishing, and hunting are basic sources of social differentiation. The same is still likely to be true, although to a lesser extent, in modern societies.

A related topic of interest here is sport and physical recreation for the disabled. Although there has been little work in this area, there has been increasing recognition of the special interests of disabled persons and the need for research. Nixon (1984b) has identified three areas of research interest: (a) identification of strategies for integration in sport activities that will be most conducive to establishing normalized relationships between disabled and nondisabled persons (see also Nixon, 1984a); (b) identification of the types and levels of sport activities that will best suit the needs and interests of the disabled; and (c) identification of ways in which competition can be structured to maximize opportunities for success and minimize the perception of failure among the disabled. In the future, it is likely that these and other questions will guide work on sport and the disabled.

Another aspect of health is mental health. There are debates regarding the extent to which mental health is biologically or socially determined. One could include this variable here on the grounds that enough evidence has accumulated that points to some genetic and physiological causation of mental illness to make this variable relevant here rather than elsewhere. However, most problems of mental health and disorder are personality problems, and organic psychoses or other clearly physiologically based mental health problems are very rare in the noninstitutionalized population usually studied. We have been able to find no studies of the impact of clearly organic kinds of mental disorder upon sport and recreational participation. The more "functional" and "psychogenic" mental problems and mental health, then, will be dealt with below, under the category of personality variables. There seems little doubt, however, that the severe organic forms of mental disorder are "limiting impairments" in the sense in which this concept was used by the ORRRC study described earlier. For hospitalized patients, as most such persons are if they have severe psychotic disorders, the chemotherapy that is pervasive in mental hospitals is likely to contribute to physiological inability or decreased ability to engage in sport and recreation, over and above the effects of the disorder itself.

One final category of health and physiological variables that bears mentioning here is one's "health history." We have found no studies relating individual health histories to current sport and recreational participation, but we would argue that such relationships are likely to be significant. Lengthy childhood illness or hospitalizations, rate of growth during childhood, one's childhood physical condition in terms of strength, coordination, and general athletic ability, the presence or absence of nonlimiting or limiting impairments during childhood and later, and the nature of one's physical self-image in terms of health (e.g., "bad heart," "sickly child") all seem relevant variables to include in the study of individual sport and recreational participation.

## Social Position and Role Factors

Under the category of social position and role we place the majority of what are usually called "demographic" or "social background" variables. They are usually important as proxy variables for sets of normative expectations associated with given roles. As noted in the introductory part of Smith and Macaulay (1980), this is true even for a number of ascribed and essentially "biosocial" variables that most social scientists tend to view as physical characteristics, such as age, gender (sex), or race. The point is not that there are no physical differences between sexes, races, and people of different ages but rather that the most important differences among people of different genders, races, or ages are not only physical. The most important differences are how these characteristics are defined and reacted to by society. In this discussion we shall consider first the biosocial variables, which are ascriptive in nature, then the nonbiosocial ascriptive social role variables (e.g., ethnicity, religion, and social class), and then the achieved, more changeable social roles such as education, income, occupation, marital status, number and ages of one's children, and one's contextual roles (as member of a given neighborhood, town, state, region, or nation).

### Birth Order

Birth order in the family of a particular individual is a biosocial role variable that has only been examined closely in recent years. It has not yet become one of the standard set of biosocial variables that social scientists routinely include in their studies. This is not surprising because birth order (especially first-born or only child versus later-born status) has been principally investigated by psychologists seeking to relate birth order to personality characteristics or attitudes rather than to behavior (see Forer, 1969; Stotland, Sherman, & Shaver, 1971). However, there has been some research in the last decade on birth order effects on sport and recreational participation. Nisbett (1968) studied 2,432 university undergraduates at three eastern U.S. universities in 1963 as well as a special sample of professional baseball and football players. Controlling for family size, it was found that firstborn individuals were less likely than later-borns to participate in sport involving physical contact or risk of significant physical injury. This result was explained in terms of earlier findings that firstborns are more reluctant to undergo or risk physical pain. Gould and Landers (1972) found similar results in terms of lesser preferences of firstborns for participation in dangerous sport as well as in less actual participation. In further support of this association, studies of male university students have shown that firstborns are more likely to avoid dangerous sport (Yiannakis, 1976) and to be underrepresented in "high harm" (Casher, 1977) sport. In contrast, Vander Velden (1971) found no association between birth order and participation in "fear" and "nonfear" sports. In studies of female intercollegiate athletes, Greendorfer (1979) found no relationship between birth order and sport participation, while Pacey (1982) found that being firstborn was positively related to sport participation.

A review of the literature on birth order by Landers (1979) shows that one general finding is that firstborns are generally high achievers, so long as the task is not dangerous or fear provoking. As Landers notes, "these findings appear to be due to maternal attention and intrusiveness toward the firstborn child" (pp. 160-161). The research also indicates that the effects of birth order are closely intertwined with those of sibling sex status. In general, girls with brothers and especially older brothers are more likely to have masculine interests, and among female athletes, those with brothers are more likely to participate in sports that are perceived to be masculine (e.g., track and field). In contrast, girls involved in feminine sports (e.g., gymnastics) are more likely to be firstborn with younger sisters and less likely to be second born with older brothers. The likely interpretation of this pattern is that it arises from a modeling effect, whereby second-born girls with older brothers are likely to adopt interests and behaviors presented by their older siblings. A final point provided by Landers in his review is that the effects of sibling sex status upon males are mixed and the research results are generally inconclusive. This may be due to the fact that for males the significance of sport in the peer culture provides the most powerful influence upon sport involvement and diminishes the importance of sibling sex status in this regard.

## Gender

Quite a few studies have been made of the general population of adults and youths regarding the relationship of gender to sport and recreational participation. In a variety of U.S. samples the same general findings have emerged: Males' participation in sport and recreation is higher than females' (Jubenville, 1971; Lundberg, Komarovsky, & McInerny, 1969; McKechnie, 1974; Standlee & Popham, 1958). Similar results have been found for one province in Canada (*Ontario Recreation Survey*, 1977; *Physical Activity Patterns in Ontario*, 1981) and in England (see Roberts, 1978). However, the broader the set of leisure measures used (covering more leisure activities than sport and recreation, including more passive forms of recreation), the more likely it is that women's participation will equal or exceed men's (see McKechnie, 1974, on crafts activities; Bishop & Ikeda, 1970, on arts and crafts, table games, picnics, and walking for pleasure; Standlee & Popham, 1958, for entertainment and hobbies; Lundberg et al., 1969, for pleasure driving). Only a few studies have shown generally equal sport and recreational participation by women (see Chapin, 1974, for a very broadly defined category of recreation and diversions; McKnelly, 1973, for how an additional hour per day of time would be used; Kenyon, 1966, for physical activity in general; see also the findings for the Canada Fitness Survey, 1983, reported later). Presumably these results reflect a dependent variable that combines nearly equal portions of active and passive recreational activities or else places less emphasis on competitive and vigorous physical activity. Corresponding results from outside the U.S. on special samples are found. For instance, Zurn (1971) sampled representatively the adult population of Cracow, Poland, and found men to be far more active in competitive sport, somewhat more active in regularized noncompetitive training, only slightly more active in irregular and haphazard sport, and about equal to females in haphazard physical exercise. Lopata (1968) found similar results with a sample of industrial workers and cooperative farmers in Czechoslovakia. And Wippler (1968) found men significantly more involved in physically active leisure in a province of the Netherlands.

Turning to the various national sample surveys conducted over the past 2 decades or so, the results are quite consistent and leave no doubt that (a) men participate much more actively (in terms of time spent and percentage engaging in an activity) in most active, vigorous sport and recreation, whereas (b) women tend to be more active than men in certain less active, less vigorous, less competitive, and less dangerous sport and recreational activities. Supporting data for this generalization are provided for the U.S. by five national surveys conducted between the late 1940s and the mid-1970s (DeGrazia, 1962; Ferris, 1970; ORRRC, 1962a, 1962c; Robinson, 1977; Sutton-Smith, Roberts, & Kozelka, 1963); for East Germany by Stockman (1974) and Wonneberger (1968); for Canada by Hobart (1975), Curtis and Milton (1973, 1976), and in a 1976 survey conducted by Statistics Canada (1978); for Denmark by Anderson et al. (1969) and Kuhl, Koch-Nielsen, and Westergaard (1966); for Norway by the Norwegian Confederation of Sport (1984), although here sex differences in overall participation are slight (52% men, 47% women); and for 12 other nations, mainly European, by Ferge et al. (1972) and Robinson (1967). The most recent research in support of these findings in North America is contained in the Miller Lite Report (1983) for the United States and in the Canada Fitness Survey (1983). Another striking finding from the Canada Fitness Survey is that, although sex differences in types of activities remain, differences in the overall level of activity have disappeared (or nearly so). In the survey, 57% of the males and 55% of the females were reported to be physically active, where activity was measured as involvement in physical recreation an average of 3 hours or more per week for 9 months or more of the year preceding the survey.

There is also evidence of regional variation in gender roles in the U.S. in one of the ORRRC studies (1962a). Although males (aged 12 and older) throughout the country were found to participate more than females in boating, camping, fishing, horse riding, hunting, outdoor games and sport, and attending outdoor sport events, females from the western U.S. were found to participate about equally or slightly more than males in hiking, swimming, waterskiing, and bicycling. Among more passive recreations, such as outdoor concerts, pleasure driving, nature walks, picnics, sightseeing, or walking for pleasure, females generally participated more, but there was approximate equality in sightseeing participation in the West, more pleasure driving by males in the Northeast, and more bicycling by males in the Northeast and South. There are probably also ethnic, religious, and class variations in the relationship of gender to sport and recreational participation. (Two studies showing social class variation were cited earlier.) But the main conclusion is that there is a great deal of consistency in the relationship of gender to sport and recreation participation although this may be changing with time.

There have been relatively few studies of the aged population (because, as will be seen below, the aged participate comparatively little in active sport and recreation). When such studies have been done, however, it has been shown that older men participate much more than older women in outdoor activities such as gardening, hunting, fishing, and other sports (Havighurst, 1961). Havighurst and Feigenbaum (1959) conclude that among older people, women show a more home-centered leisure style and less leisure than men, with socioeconomic status held constant.

## Age

Age has a generally clear and consistent relationship to sport and outdoor recreational participation in a wide range of studies, both in the United States and elsewhere. Although there are few studies of really young children to tell us about that extreme end of the age continuum, the overwhelming conclusion from empirical research on the subject is that recreational and sport participation tends to decline with age (at least from adolescence on). The rapidity of the decline varies with the kind of activity involved. The more strenuous sport and recreational activities, requiring greater physical stamina and prowess, tend to decline with age much more rapidly than the less strenuous activities (though not necessarily or only because of declining physical powers). Many of the latter decline rather slowly with age (for instance, golf, tennis, fishing, hiking, camping, nature or bird walks, walking for pleasure in general, and driving for pleasure) until about age 50 or so, when the decline tends to quicken for several of these. This decline with age is not uniform across countries and samples. Some special samples show declines with age until the mid-20s, then increases in participation in the late 20s and early 30s, followed by decline. Also, in some special samples (for instance, American retirement communities with a relatively homogeneous, high-status population), we often see an increase in less strenuous sport and recreational participation immediately after retirement, followed by the usual decline with advancing age. The fact that the relationship of age to sport and outdoor recreational participation is relatively uniform for almost all sport and outdoor recreational activities indicates that more than simple declining physical prowess is at work. Although no studies we are aware of investigate age-role expectations regarding sport and outdoor recreation, existing data suggest that normative expectations are at least as important in this decline as are physical and physiological factors. Clearly we need some research directly focused on age-role norms and expectations regarding sport and outdoor recreational activities.

The empirical literature supporting these broad generalizations includes data from various U.S. samples, both haphazardly and purposely gathered, showing a decline in sport and outdoor recreational participation with age. These samples include high school students (Witt, 1971), relatively high-status members of retirement communities (Bultena & Wood, 1970), zoo-goers (Cheek, 1971a), and university alumni (Chrouser, 1973). Walking for pleasure, gardening, and shuffleboard are outdoor recreations that sometimes have shown an increase with age, as have indoor recreational activities like square dancing, social dancing, and indoor table games, hobbies, and crafts; a study of wilderness hiking party leaders yielded no significant age effect (Jubenville, 1971). However, a number of more methodologically sound samples of single American cities or states have supported the broad generalizations made above (Havighurst, 1957, 1961; Havighurst & Feigenbaum, 1959; Kenyon, 1966; McKechnie, 1974; Snyder & Spreitzer, 1974; Spreitzer & Snyder, 1983; Unkel, 1981). When the dependent variable is a broad recreation index, including both passive and active, indoor and outdoor recreational activities, there is a tendency for age to show a curvilinear relationship with a peak at between 35-50 years of age (Christensen & Yoesting, 1973; Reich, 1965). The decline with age is less for cognitive (mass media sport attention) than for behavioral (participatory) and affective (emotional) involvement, particularly for men (Snyder & Spreitzer, 1974). The decline is also less for watching, listening to, or attending sport events than for actual participation (Kenyon, 1966).

Full national sample surveys at different points in time in the U.S. also give solid confirmation of the generalization stated. These include the large national sample surveys by ORRRC of the adolescent and adult population, one of them including data from respondents at different seasons of the year conducted in 1960-1961, and another follow-up study in 1965 (ORRRC, 1962a,b,c). Both the plots of simple frequency distributions and more complex multivariate analyses show a steady decline of outdoor sport and recreational participation with age. (See also Cicchetti, 1972; Ferris, 1970.) However, data from a national U.S. urban sample reported by Robinson (1977) indicated a big decline in sport participation after age 20, followed by a more gradual decline until about age 50, when the decline again became much sharper. Sport event attendance showed a similar pattern, as did pleasure driving, in the DeGrazia (1962) study, but working around the yard and in the garden showed a gradual increase with age. This last finding is especially important in again suggesting the importance of age-role norms as causative factors, rather than physiological factors associated with age. Most recently, the Miller Lite Survey (1983) reported declining participation in sport with age, with particularly striking changes at age 50 and again at age 65.

Data from other nations yield markedly similar patterns to those seen with U.S. data. Various purposive and haphazard samples from Poland (Wohl, 1969), England and Canada (Hall, 1973), France (Dumazedier, 1973), Czechoslovakia (Lopata, 1968), Denmark (Riiskjar, 1984), and the Netherlands (Rijsdorp, 1960), as well as Luschen's (1967) conclusions from his review of the literature, support the generalization that the greatest participation in sport and outdoor recreation is seen among youth, with a decline in such activity with increasing age. Even among schoolchildren in the 6th, 8th, and 11th grades in Finnish and Midwest U.S. schools, a decline in overall participation in sport with age (Iso-Ahola, 1975) was seen. Samples of whole cities or provinces (or the equivalent) outside the U.S. show similarly consistent results: These include random samples of the populations of Groningen, the Netherlands (Wippler, 1968), Cracow, Poland (Zurn, 1971), a Finnish town (Heinila, 1959), and the Canadian provinces of Alberta (Hobart, 1975) and Ontario (*Ontario Recreation Survey*, 1977; *Physical Activity Pat-*

*terns in Ontario,* 1981) in which sport and outdoor recreational participation decline with age, as does recreational physical activity in general. The only variation in this pattern was reported by Lopata (1968), this being an increase in the late 20s and early 30s, followed and preceded by the usual decline with age.

The results from national sample surveys outside the U.S. are essentially the same. In Denmark (Anderson et al., 1969; Kuhl et al., 1966), Norway (Norwegian Confederation of Sport, 1984), Canada (Curtis & Milton, 1973, 1976; Hobart, 1975; McPherson & Kozlik, 1979; White, 1975), and 10 other nations, mainly European plus the U.S. (Robinson, 1967), less sport activity and physical exercise is seen with advancing age. Anderson and others (1969) also reported an age decline in reading about or listening to media sport, a peak in sport involvement around 15-25 years of age, and a sharp decline after age 55 in sport and athletic participation. Kuhl et al. (1966) found the decline in Danish sport participation particularly marked after age 30, but also reported reversals in this trend for a few sport and outdoor recreation types (fishing, hunting, tennis, sailing), at least through middle age. The 1972 Canadian data reported by Milton (1976) showed declines with age in physical recreation, number of sports participated in, specific sport participation, and even spectatorship at sport events. This pattern held up when statistical controls for other sociodemographic variables were applied. Similarly, the analysis of 1976 Canadian national survey data by McPherson and Kozlik (1979) showed a pattern of declining involvement in sport and physical activity with age (see also Statistics Canada, 1978). This pattern was repeated in the Canada Fitness Survey (1983). An interesting finding for Canadian participants was reported by Curtis and White (1984) in their analysis of the 1976 data. This analysis showed that, while age is inversely related to involvement in sport and physical recreation, the intensity of involvement in particular activities (measured by frequency) increased with age for sport participants. Curtis and White interpret the findings to suggest that sport participants do not relinquish their inclinations to participate with age. Rather, they change the nature of their participation by reducing the number of different activities they are involved in but intensifying their involvement in these fewer activities. In the Szalai multination study (reported by Robinson, 1967), the decline in sport participation was seen most sharply by men after 50 years of age and for women after 30 years of age. This varied somewhat by country, with some peaks in the 30- to 60-year range. Education was controlled in the U.S. sample; this made the age-decline relationship stronger. However, the amount of time spent on sport and active recreation is so small (averaging only minutes per day) that trends for particular countries are hard to detect. The most reliable results from the 10-nation study, then, are the average peak participation ages for women and men described above and the general decline in participation with increasing age.

Although the general impact of age upon sport and recreational participation is clear, we know almost nothing about the extent to which age role expectations in different countries shape the observed patterns. Rapoport and Rapoport (1975) coined the term "enjoyment career" to suggest that different types of leisure activities have different age profiles. Lifespan time allocation studies are needed to investigate this suggestion properly, rather than cross-sectional studies, because cultural, social structural, and other contextual changes could otherwise not be separated out as determinants. The role of physical self-image as contrasted with actual physiological condition should also be investigated in order to understand better the observed general decline in sport and physical activity with age. It is likely that the observed decline of physical recreation with age accelerates far faster than the decline in actual physiological abilities to participate (recall the increase in gardening and some indoor recreation with age). One causative factor may be the emphasis on competition in sport, which appeals most to the young, instead of an emphasis on physical recreation for fun and maintenance of health. These emphases may vary markedly by culture and subculture, and such variations should be studied carefully. Finally, it is important to have more studies that not only focus on composite indices of many different sports but also focus on comparisons of indoor physical recreation versus outdoor, competitive versus noncompetitive physical recreation, strenuous versus nonstrenuous physical recreation, and other such analytical distinctions, as well as on single sports or specific types of physical recreation. In some cases, the composite indices reflect mainly the patterns for popular sports and recreations, which means that dissimilar patterns in less popular sports are obscured. Robinson (1967) suggests that this may be the case in the United States; in particular he believes that the very popular activities of bowling and physical exercising (calisthenics, physical fitness exercises) should not be included in composite indices of sport and recreational activities but rather analyzed separately.

## Race

Racial differences have rarely been studied in the field of sport and outdoor recreation participation by amateurs. Brown (1976) notes that few black social scientists are concerned with the relationship of race to sport involvement, most preferring to look at more "substantial" problems. He argues that, in America at least, the notion of black and white equality in athletics is a myth. Indeed, Brown suggests that what is needed is a research focus specifically on these myths and their impact, as well as on the general impact of subcultural roles and stereotypes on sport and recreational participation. Loy (1976) also calls for more research in this area and suggests specifically that there be more focus on changes over time in the relationship between race and sport participation, as well as on the types of assimilation of blacks into sport and recreational participation in America. One of the earliest accounts of black recreational activity was provided by Myrdal (1969) in his classic analysis of the social life of U.S. blacks, *An American Dilemma*. His discussion emphasizes that because of the lack of facilities, recreation tends to be informal and unorganized. Additional historical accounts are provided by Edwards (1969) and McPherson (1976). Edwards provides a brief overview of black participation in sport and develops a more extensive discussion of the place of athletics in the black colleges. McPherson (1976) reviews the history of black athletes in America, noting that until very recently there has been very powerful discrimination against blacks and other darker skinned persons in major sports. Based largely on impressionistic evidence, he argues that blacks have long been very active in amateur sport in America but usually within black groups, teams, and leagues. He also notes that blacks have been most involved in sports requiring less expensive facilities and equipment (track and field, baseball) or that express aggression (boxing, wrestling, judo, karate, weight training). In his view, current cultural expectations for blacks are that they will excel in sport. The civil rights and black power movements of the 1960s and early 1970s in the U.S. have made an impact in opening up organized sport, including professional sport, to blacks. Curry and Jiobu (1984) provide further insight on the history of blacks in sport, noting the parallels between cycles of segregation and discrimination in sport and practices in broader American society.

But what of empirical research on the subject? Sadly, there is very little, comparatively speaking, and it fails to investigate the importance of role expectations, as is true with other kinds of sociodemographic variable research. With a sample of Washington, DC, adults, Chapin (1974) reports that whites participate more than blacks in terms of a composite index of recreation and other diversions. Unfortunately, this dependent variable is much broader than our focus here, and the results do not control for the crucial factor of socioeconomic status, which could readily account for the observed results (as could also be true in a Finnish student study by Iso-Ahola, 1975). With data from the Barbados (West Indies), however, Martindale (1971) does show significant black-white differences in sport participation with socioeconomic status controlled, studying 500 tenth-grade boys.

The major national sample surveys in the U.S. including race role (black-white) as a variable have confirmed generally lower black participation in sport and outdoor recreational activities in general than for whites, with other sociodemographic variables controlled (see Cicchetti, 1972; Ferris, 1970; Kaplan, 1960; ORRRC, 1962a, b; Robinson, 1977). These analyses suggest continuing racial discrimination effects that depress black people's sport and outdoor recreational participation in the U.S., or else a different (lower) preference for such activities by U.S. blacks, which sounds like a rationalization (see Seneca, Davidson, & Adams, 1968). There are some kinds of activities in which black participation exceeded white participation in the 1960-1961 ORRRC national survey, namely, active recreation, but this difference had essentially vanished by the time of the 1965 national survey (Ferris, 1970).

Luschen (1967) suggests that blacks often choose to participate in competitive sport in order to attain social mobility, being less able to attain it in other spheres. He further suggests that blacks attempt such social mobility in certain sports where discrimination against them is more difficult (for instance, boxing, track, baseball) because there is objective evaluation of results, individual performance, and little power over others involved (see Blalock, 1962). Such sports can also be practiced with little financial investment or resources required, so that black youth can begin them at an early age even if poor or discriminated against at local recreational facilities. This kind of explanation has yet to be tested adequately, so far as we know, and would mainly apply to a small percentage of blacks. For the large majority of blacks in the U.S., and for other dark-skinned minorities in the U.S. and elsewhere, the explanation for lesser participation in sport and recreational activities is likely to be found in both lower economic status (resulting from long-term discrimination against them), which constricts the individual's resource opportunity structure, as well as in the general discrimination against such persons at recreational sites and facilities. In short, the stigmatized role of dark-skinned minority persons in white societies is the probable principal determinant. Research on both black *and* white role expectations regarding sport and recreational activities of both blacks and whites is much needed because to our knowledge none exists.

## Religion

Religious roles have received even less attention than racial roles in the study of sport, though there are fewer theoretical reasons why religious roles might be important in this sphere. Several authors have discussed the historical association between religion and the rise of sport and recreational activity. Many athletic activities began as religious rites (Brasch, 1970; see Sage, 1980). Loy, McPherson, and Kenyon (1978) note that until the Middle Ages leisure activities were under the control of the church, and sporting competitions were held only in conjunction with religious observances and holidays. During the Middle Ages, sporting activities began to be pursued apart from religious sponsorship, but the influence of the church remained strong. In North America, this was a result of Christianity's emphasis on the primacy of the mind over the body, which resulted in a de-emphasis on or discouraging of sport and play and was evident in regulations such as those banning competition on Sunday. The relationship between the church and leisure institutions changed in the 20th century, which saw a rise in the standard of living and increased leisure time and recreational participation. In response to these changing conditions, the church began to re-exert its influence by supporting sport and recreational activities as healthy and beneficial and even sponsoring recreational and sporting events (Loy et al., 1978; Sage, 1980).

Kaplan (1960) has discussed the possible role of religion in affecting leisure participation, stressing the possible importance of the Calvinist Protestant ethic. And we have already mentioned Luschen's (1964) suggestion that Protestantism is likely to be associated with higher sport performance because of the association of Protestantism with an achievement ethic. However, when one looks at the meager data available, this explanation does not seem to hold up. Wippler (1968), in his study of Groningen, Netherlands, found that being Catholic (rather than having no church or being Protestant) was significantly associated with outdoor (vs. indoor) leisure behavior and with a dynamic-expansive leisure pattern (which involved active sports, swimming, dancing, and voluntary association participation), even with other sociodemographic variables controlled. In his U.S. study, Robinson (1977) similarly found Catholics more active in sport. Gruneau (1976), however, found that Protestants were overrepresented and Catholics underrepresented among members of provincial sport teams in Canada. Obviously, much more research is needed on the impact of religious roles upon sport and recreational participation before we can begin to approach an understanding of their impact. The major national sample surveys in the U.S. and elsewhere have simply ignored the religious roles of individuals as factors in such participation. And not only do indicators of religious role incumbency need to be included, but also there must be some investigation of how religious role norms relate to sport and recreational participation, if at all, for a given religious role in a given time and society or subculture.

## Employment

Employment status (being employed versus being a housewife or unemployed) has received relatively little attention in the research literature on sport and outdoor recreational participation, but there are several relevant studies nonetheless. The general results are mixed, varying according to the nature of the dependent variable or activity index used. On the whole, however, the employed (and nearly all studies concern employed vs. not-employed *women*) tend to participate more in sport but less in other outdoor activities. This is shown most clearly by Ferge et al. (1972) with the data of the Szalai et al. (1972) 12-nation study. Ten of the 12 nations' data support the foregoing generalizations. More refined analysis of the U.S. data from that multinational study confirms these results, particularly Robinson (1977), as does an earlier national survey of the U.S. reported by DeGrazia (1962). The latter study sheds light on why there might be the discrepancy between these two types of outdoor recreation, for it in fact compared involvement in sport, attending sport events, and gardening rather than some catchall "other outdoor activities" category. A national survey of the German Democratic Republic (East Germany) as reported by Stockman (1974) shows similar results: Employed women were more involved in a broad category of activity including sport, culture, and entertainment, while not-employed women were more involved in gardening, walking for pleasure, passive recreation, and "other leisure activities" (the employed women also being more involved in social activities, adult education, and reading newspapers and magazines).

The studies with samples of smaller geographical scope show more mixed results, but on the whole the generalization made above seems to hold. Lundberg et al. (1969), in their early (1930s) study of leisure in Westchester County, a Connecticut suburb of New York City, found employed women more active than not-employed women in both sport and motoring (no measure of gardening or pleasure walking being included in the report). Similarly, McKnelly (1973) found higher recreational participation among the employed than among the not-employed (mainly housewives), with data from random samples of adults 18 and older in seven Texas counties. In a study of three towns in Washington state, Nye (1958) found no difference between employed and unemployed mothers in terms of their participation in sport, recreation, dancing, and movie attendance (a combined index of recreational activity). Mihovilovic's (1973) study of married women in 15 Yugoslavian towns (using data provided by their husbands) is a still greater, though methodologically less sound, exception to the generalization made earlier. He found the housewives to spend more time than the employed women in walking, gardening, and sport (though only by a few minutes per day for the latter). And in his study of Washington, DC, Chapin (1974) found the unemployed and not-employed, males and females combined, to participate significantly more in "recreation" and "other diversions"—an omnibus category that does not let us differentiate between sport and active recreation versus more passive indoor or outdoor leisure activities.

Thus, although there are a few contradictory or potentially contradictory results, the general conclusion is clear that the employed are more likely to participate in sport and active outdoor recreation than the not-employed, particularly housewives. The latter, on the other hand, are more likely to be involved in relatively inactive outdoor recreation such as walking for pleasure or gardening. Note the similarity of the latter findings to the findings regarding age. The not-employed tend to show a sport and recreation pattern rather like that of the aged, while the employed tend to show a pattern more like the young. We shall later argue that this similarity has meaning in the larger context of the General Activity Pattern (described by the General Activity Model mentioned in chapter one). In any event, more research is needed on the normative role expectations that accompany employed versus not-employed or unemployed (in the labor force but lack a job) status as they bear on sport and recreational participation. Some facts on the effect of employment status upon sport and recreational participation are clear (though generally only in bivariate form, without controls for other sociodemographic variables), but their meaning is unclear.

## Discretionary Time

Free time or discretionary time available to an individual is a potentially important social role variable. It is the result of subtracting the time required by obligatory or semi-obligatory roles and activities from the total time budget of an individual. Various studies make it clear, not surprisingly, that the not-employed or unemployed have more free time (Chapin, 1974, p. 114; Lundberg et al., 1969; McKnelly, 1973; Mihovilovic, 1973; Robinson, 1977; Stockman, 1974; Wippler, 1968, p. 152a). The data from the 12-nation Szalai et al. (1972) study are completely consistent on this point when employed women and housewives are compared for workdays, with differences ranging from about 30 minutes to 2 hours per day, on the average, depending on the country involved (Ferge et al., 1972). However, the data reviewed in the previous paragraphs make it clear that this additional free time is not primarily used for additional sport and outdoor recreational activities of an active sort. McKnelly (1973) states unequivocally that those with the greatest amounts of free time are *least* likely to be active recreational participants, based on his study of the adults in seven Texas counties. This lack of a direct relationship between amount of free time and sport and outdoor recreational activities is not surprising in view of the fact that the latter activities constitute a very small percentage of total free time of most individuals. Robinson (1977) indicates for a U.S. urban national sample that only 2-5% of total leisure is devoted to active sport and outdoor activities. More broadly, Robinson, Converse, and Szalai (1972) indicate that active sport and outdoor recreational activities together account generally for less than 10-15% of total leisure time in the data from all 12 countries studied by Szalai et al. (1972).

Thus, at the very least, the relationship between free time and sport and outdoor recreation is problematic. In a Multiple Classification Analysis of time budget data from the U.S., Robinson (1977) indicated the major sociodemographic determinants of free time for both men and women separately. For men, the outstanding factors were employment status and day of the week (with Sundays being by far the greatest day of free time—4 times as much as Saturday). Other important factors for his sample of men aged 18-59 were youth (being aged 18-29), being Catholic, being not married, being childless, having more children over 4 years of age, living in rural fringe areas or smaller urban places, and having either very low or very high income. For women, the same kind of analysis and data showed only day of the week to be a really outstanding factor (again Sunday being many times more a day of free time than Saturday, and the latter more than a weekday). Other factors making for more free time for women included having ''some college'' as an educational level, being younger (18-29 years), being black, being Jewish or of an established Protestant denomination, not being employed (second in strength after day of the week), being not married, having no children, very poor weather, and having a high or moderately low (not extremely low) income. There are other factors that also affect the amount of leisure time, doubtless, but also factors that affect the *usefulness* of free time.

Blakelock (1960) has done some seminal work in this area, pointing out that the amount of free time is quite different from its ''liquidity,'' by which he refers to the degree to which free time can be used for a variety of activities. Free time in the hours from 1:00 to 5:00 in the morning has low liquidity, because there are relatively few leisure activities one can usually engage in at such times—most commercial recreation sites are closed, most people with normal daily work and play schedules are asleep, and there are laws to enforce quietness, sometimes even a curfew to restrict spatial mobility. By contrast, the same amount of free time from 1:00 to 5:00 in the afternoon of a Saturday or Sunday has great liquidity because a wide variety of alternative activities can be engaged in as discretionary activity. Blakelock also notes that activities can be similarly classified according to their degree of timing flexibility: Some activities can only, by custom, be performed at certain, perhaps even unique, times (for instance, one's paid job, attending a concert, going to church services); other activities can be performed almost anytime (visiting or talking with friends or family, for instance). Ferge et al. (1972) show this in detail for data from 12 nations. Finally, Blakelock notes that the least flexible obligatory activities structure one's other activities, which must be fitted around them. "If the least flexible activities take up an individual's time of greatest liquidity, he may be relatively poor in time. The night worker gives an example of this" (p. 452). Blakelock also introduces two additional dimensions of individual time use: rigidity of the total time budget, which refers to the degree to which new activities can be fit in or existing activities shifted around in their position; and harmony of the time budget, which refers to the degree of appropriate matchup between activity opportunities and the individual's interest in engaging in such activities. Empirical data gathered from rotating shift workers and regular daytime workers in a large U.S. oil refinery indicate that, as predicted, shift workers tend to engage more in flexible leisure time activities such as working around the house or yard and garden rather than engaging in voluntary organization activity or visiting friends (Blakelock, 1960). No measure of sport participation was included. However, Robinson (1977) shows for a national U.S. urban sample that although shift work is not related to active sport, employed men who do shift work are significantly more likely to engage in outdoor recreational activities (including gardening in this category), while employed women doing shift work are significantly *less* likely to do so. A somewhat related study by McEvoy (1974) suggests a 4-day, 40-hour work week would significantly increase outdoor recreation. Clearly more study of the effect of free time liquidity and the effects of shift work on sport and outdoor recreational activity is needed, again with some attention to the normative expectations involved regarding when during the day various kinds of activities should or should not be performed.

The empirical evidence on the earlier point regarding the effect of amount of free time on sport and outdoor recreational activity is mixed. In the U.S., Witt (1971) found that hours of work were positively associated with a sport participation factor among high school students, suggesting less free time is associated with active sport participation. However, on another factor dealing with outdoor nature activities, no such relationship was found. Mihovilovic (1973), in a study of 15 Yugoslavian towns, found greater free time associated both with more sport participation and with other outdoor recreational activities (gardening, walking for pleasure) among married women. Heinila (1959) similarly found more physical exercise among his sample from a Finnish town for persons with more leisure time, and Wippler (1968) found more outdoor leisure activity with more free time in his study of Groningen, Netherlands (though there was no effect on physically active vs. passive leisure). Further, with data from a Canadian national sample of adults, Hobart (1975) reports that greater free time is associated with more active sport participation for both men and women in different age groups. However, when a multiple regression analysis was performed, free time showed significant strength as a predictor of sport participation only for men under 35 years and over 54 years of age. And in Groves and Kahalas' (1975) study of users of a U.S. wild game (animals) recreation area, they found both "free time" (discretionary time) and "leisure time" (time spent participating in activities of interest) to be significantly related to outdoor activities and forest recreation, but they concluded that the relationship was only a weak one. Their interpretation, based on a rotated factor analysis, was that some people in the general population are location-specific in their outdoor recreation (in this case, concentrating on the game lands area studied), others are activity-specific in their choice of recreation (in this case, engaging in recreation in public forested areas but not necessarily any specific area), while still others spend their leisure time in ways that do not involve either a specific outdoor recreation area or even outdoor recreation in forested areas more generally. This study is particularly valuable as a prototype of what might be done for the whole range of sport and outdoor recreational activities, preferably with more extensive samples. It suggests that people in general may tend to have site-specific outdoor sport and recreational preferences, to have activity-specific outdoor sport and recreational preferences, or to be rather eclectic in both site and activity choices regarding outdoor sport and recreation. The latter preference pattern, with extensive substitutability of both sites and activities, begins to sound very much like part of a General Activity Pattern (described by the General Activity Model mentioned in chapter one). Thus, future research must focus in sharply on the extent to which the three kinds of patterns suggested exist generally in the population and on how these patterns relate to the General Activity Pattern. Note, too, that the foregoing research approach appropriately involves activity sites as well as activity types abstracted from their behavior setting.

Two other aspects of the relationship of free time to sport and recreational participation have received a small amount of study. Cottrell (1961) has suggested that one major source of additional free time in modern industrial society is increased longevity. And Bultena and Wood (1970) have shown that, indeed, sport and recreational activities do tend to increase after retirement to a higher status U.S. retirement community, though these activities then again continue their decline with age. Additional studies on the effects of retirement on sport and outdoor recreational participation would be welcome. It is quite possible that the foregoing findings are an artifact of the special sample studied, and special norms encourage such participation in U.S. retirement community inhabitants. The other factor related to free time that has received some attention is the matter of vacation time from work, including both regular days off as well as longer vacations. There are very few studies of either aspect of vacation time, perhaps because researchers consider the variables too "obvious" for inclusion in their studies. Data from the Szalai et al. (1972) multination study indicate, as one would expect, that sport and outdoor recreational activity are more frequent on weekend days, particularly Sundays (Robinson, 1967). Similarly, greater outdoor recreational activity was associated with weekend days for both men and women in Robinson's (1977) analysis of a national U.S. urban sample from the prior multination sample, but active sport participation, surprisingly, was *not* so related. In fact, for men there was a small negative relationship between sport activity and weekend days. Chapin's (1974) data for Washington, DC indicate more sport and recreation on weekends.

The data for vacations of the longer sort are clearer: The ORRRC (1962b) found from U.S. national sample data that outdoor recreation and sport activity was significantly associated with the length of one's paid vacation each year, those having 2 or more weeks of paid vacation being much more likely to engage in such activity even with many other sociodemographic factors controlled. However, the relationship was weaker for employed women than for men and was nonsignificant for *all* women when other sociodemographic variables were controlled. The association of longer vacations with sport and outdoor recreational participation suggests that, unless an employed person has more than a minimal amount of annual vacation time (that is, more than a week) available, the individual will use that time for other activities than outdoor sport and active recreation—perhaps for work around the house, yard, and garden or else indoor recreation, rest, and relaxation. Again, more research is needed here as elsewhere to understand the meaning of short versus longer annual paid vacation periods, as well as the meaning of days off from work and weekend days in relation to normative expectations for sport and outdoor recreational participation. That free time is ultimately an important factor in sport and outdoor recreational participation in people's minds is clearly demonstrated by the fact that the major U.S. national sample surveys of outdoor recreation in the 1960s (see Cicchetti, 1972) show consistently that 55-60% of the reasons for not participating as often as one would like in favorite outdoor recreation activities and 25-30% of reasons given for not participating at all in a desired outdoor recreational activity involve lack of time owing to family or work responsibilities or other time constraints. Similar results have been obtained in Canadian surveys. Respondents to the Statistics Canada Survey of Fitness, Physical Recreation and Sport (Statistics Canada, 1978), to the Canada Fitness Survey (1983), and to the *Ontario Recreation Survey* (1977) most often indicated that the main reason preventing their increased participation in these activities was lack of time. Finally, respondents to the Norwegian Confederation of Sport survey (1984) indicated that lack of time was the most common reason for not participating in physical activity.

## Marital Status

Marital status and its corresponding role expectations (the latter, of course, never directly investigated in relation to leisure activity) are another factor in sport and recreational participation. Because of the interaction of this variable with other life cycle stage variables (such as number and age of children, age of the individual and spouse, etc.), analyses of its effects on physical recreation have produced mixed results. Some studies with purposive samples (Standlee & Popham, 1958, with Indian schoolteachers; Hall, 1973, with English and some Canadian women) show mixed results, with no relation of marital status to sport participation in the first case and a decline in such participation upon marriage (for women) in the second. Two random samples of a broader sort (Wippler, 1968, of the province of Groningen, Netherlands; and Heinila, 1959, of a Finnish town) show similar mixed results: no relationship of marital status to outdoor or physical leisure activities in the first case, but more physical exercise if single in the second case. The former result is more compelling, however, since it emerges from a multivariate analysis controlling other sociodemographic variables. Wippler (1968) did, however, find being single was associated with the factor he called dynamic expansiveness, which is a composite of sport participation , swimming, sport spectatorship, dancing, movie attendance, and attendance at association meetings. Even more confidence must be put in national sample surveys and cross-national surveys, though their results need careful interpretation.

The problem is that the relationship of marital status with sport and recreational participation looks different on the surface than it actually is when appropriate controls for confounding sex and life cycle stage variables are introduced. While Robinson (1977) finds there is no apparent relationship of marital status to active sport or outdoor recreational participation, separate examination of males and employed and unemployed females shows clear relationships, though complex ones. For employed males, not-married status is significantly associated with active sport participation but is negatively and significantly associated with outdoor recreation of other sorts. For employed females, not-married status was also significantly negatively associated with outdoor recreation, but there was no relation at all with sport participation. For not-employed females, the relationships are quite reversed: The not-married are significantly more involved in outdoor recreation other than sport and significantly less involved in active sport.

The earlier national U.S. survey of the ORRRC (1962a) found no effect of single versus married status on any of four indices of outdoor recreation (passive pursuits, water related, backwoods, or active outdoor recreation, including sport). These results emerged from a multi-variate analysis that was done separately for men and women and that controlled for various other sociodemographic variables. Hence one must conclude that other studies finding apparent effects of marital status, at least in the U.S., are instead finding artifacts of other confounded variables. Canadian national sample data, as reported by Hobart (1975) and by Curtis and Milton (1976), further contribute to the complexity here. Although there is no apparent general effect of marital status on sport and outdoor recreational participation, there is participation in a greater number of sports to a moderate extent for married persons (even controlling for sex, age, and education).

In the multinational data reported by Ferge et al. (1972), both active sport and other outdoor recreation are generally higher for unemployed males and females in two thirds of the countries studied, with the relationships of married and unmarried very close or equal in all but one of the other countries. But for not-employed women the results are much more mixed. Further analysis of the Canadian 1972 national sample data (Curtis & Milton, 1976; Hobart, 1975) shows that clearer results emerge when the data are analyzed separately by sex and age groupings. Here it is found that the single are more active in sport participation whether male or female if under 35 years of age, even with controls for other variables involved. By contrast, males over age 35 are more active on all sport and recreation indices if married. In the analysis of the 1976 Canadian national sample survey reported by Statistics Canada (1976), single persons had higher rates of participation in all categories of activity examined, including participation in any sport and in eight specific sports (swimming, ice skating, tennis, golf, ice hockey, cross-country skiing, and curling). Similar patterns of higher participation rates among single persons were found in the

Canada Fitness Survey (1983) and in a survey of the Norwegian population (Norwegian Confederation of Sport, 1984).

Further information on the relationship between physical activity and marital status has been provided in a recent multivariate analysis of the 1976 Canadian survey for one activity. Brown and Curtis (1984) examined the characteristics of those persons who indicated that they had participated in running or jogging during the month preceding the survey. Their analysis showed that in proportion to their representation in the general population, married persons were underrepresented among male and female runners and in all age categories. When age was controlled, the pattern held for males with no postsecondary education and males and females with postsecondary education, while married persons were not underrepresented among female runners with no postsecondary education. The pattern of underrepresentation of married persons persisted when the sample was divided into high and low intensity runners (high intensity defined as regularly spending more than 60 minutes running on each occasion) and high and low frequency runners (high frequency measured as participating 28 or more times in the previous month). In a related study, McTeer and Curtis (1984) found in surveys of participants in two marathon races in Canada that married persons were underrepresented among female marathoners but not among male marathoners.

The net conclusion of all this must be that there is some tendency for the single to participate more in sport and outdoor recreation. It is possible also that some other variables dealing with the nature of one's family (number and ages of children) and life cycle stage are more basic than marital status in this complex of relationships with sport and recreational participation. At the very least, there is strong need for research that studies specifically the role expectations of single, married, divorced, separated, widowed, and cohabiting persons with regard to sport and recreational participation. We should not be content with the married-unmarried status measure as a proxy and pile up more research that will not help us to understand the meaning of marital status in this context.

## Family Composition

Family size and age composition are two complex status variables that form part of the larger life cycle stage set of variables. Again the results are mixed, both because many studies fail to introduce appropriate controls for possibly confounding variables (socioeconomic status, age, marital status, length of marriage) and because there is little or no investigation of the social meaning of large and small family size, or of having younger or older children. Thus, Nisbett (1968) finds that students from larger families in several colleges tend to play more dangerous sports, whereas Wippler (1968), in his sample of the adults of the province of Groningen, Netherlands, finds no family size effects on sport and outdoor recreational participation when other sociodemographic and some related attitude variables are controlled. In Denmark, however, Riiskjar (1984) reports from a survey of the adult population in the city of Ringsted that women without children have a participation level more than 10 times as high as women with children. More confidence may be placed in two national sample surveys from the U.S. that dealt with family size as a variable. The first study, reported by Robinson (1977), with no statistical controls for other variables, finds larger families associated with less active sport participation for employed males (fathers of the children) but more participation in other outdoor recreation. For employed females these relationships are exactly reversed, with significantly more active sport and less other outdoor recreation. And for the not-employed females, larger numbers of children are associated with both more sport and more other outdoor recreational participation.

The second national U.S. study, by the ORRRC (1962a), is better by virtue of involving a multivariate analysis controlling for several other sociodemographic variables, including age, marital status, and employment status. These results show some evidence of "child impedance" or the hindering effect of the age of the youngest child, rather than family size per se (which is not included in the data). Specifically, having children under 5 years of age is associated with less participation in passive outdoor recreation among females from the South, less participation in water-related outdoor recreation in females from the Northeast, and more involvement in active outdoor recreation (particularly sport) among females from the Northeast and North Central regions of the U.S. Having younger children also led to more involvement in backwoods outdoor recreation for males in the South. Other studies without statistical controls also show some effects of child impedance (having young children)—Cheek (1971a), and Sessoms (1963), for instance (though White, 1975, finds no family size effect, children's age not considered). And Robinson's (1977) national urban U.S. sample data also evidence such younger child impedance, but in a mixed way: Employed males with young children were less involved in other outdoor recreation, but this factor had no effect on sport participation; employed females were significantly less active both in sport and other outdoor recreation; while not-employed females were more involved in other outdoor recreation and less involved in sport. Hence, there is evidence for a hindering effect of younger children, but it varies by sex, employment status, type of outdoor recreation, and probably age. Simple family size measures thus may or may not show the child impedance effect. Finally, in Norway, the national survey conducted by the Norwegian Confederation of Sport (1984) found that persons with older children (13 years old or older) are more active than those with younger children, although those who have children are, on the average, more physically active than those who do not.

## Life Cycle Stage and Family Roles

Life cycle stage and family role constellation are two roughly similar broad variables that attempt to incorporate and make some sense out of the otherwise confusing welter of mixed relationships one generally finds between a dependent social behavior variable and such single predictors as age, sex, employment status, marital status, number of children, age composition of children, length of marriage, and so on. The basic notion is that there is so much interaction among such family life variables that only a complex typological variable can do justice to their effects, unless extremely complex nonlinear multivariate analysis is used. The importance of the family role constellation and life cycle stage is unquestionable, especially because it involves age, a variable that we have previously seen is very important in understanding sport and outdoor recreational participation. Angrist (1967), studying some American university alumnae, used a family role constellation approach to show that for both spectator sport and bowling (the only other sport included), participation was least for women who were married, who were not working at a paid job, and who had preschool children. Willmott (1971), studying married male employees from two manufacturing firms in England, showed that 60% of men's out-of-the-home (and presumably often outdoors) recreational activities were with family members, whether wife or children. And Orthner (1975), studying an upper-middle-class sample from a Southeastern U.S. city, found that the degree of individual, joint (involving mutual spouse interaction), and parallel (involving the spouses in the same place and time but not interacting) recreational activities varied according to life cycle stage. Joint recreational activities were particularly more frequent early in the marriage and then again later in the marriage (and were related to shared marital communication, Orthner, 1976), while individual recreational activities became common only after the first 5 years of marriage, and parallel activities were common throughout.

Another analysis of the effects of family life cycle stage upon leisure activities was conducted by Kelly (1975). With data collected from 138 adults in a Western university town and a Midwestern industrial town,

Kelly found support for a proposed four-phase leisure cycle for adults. Prior to marriage, leisure activities are unconditioned or chosen primarily for their intrinsic value and satisfaction. Married adults who are childless have leisure styles much like those not married, except that they more often engage in recreation together. Parenthood results in a movement toward complementary activities that are performed with other family members and are associated with parental role obligations. The period between the time that the last child leaves home and retirement combines unconditional and complementary activities almost evenly.

All of this suggests that we really know very little about how the whole set of family life and role variables affects sport and recreational participation. Even the ORRRC (1962b), with multivariate analysis controls, tells us very little when we find that for a U.S. national sample outdoor recreation in general is higher for single persons under 45 years of age, for married persons with school-age children, and for married persons under 45 years with no children. All that is clear is a child impedance effect. But we know next to nothing about how to sort out the effects of the rest of the variables discussed in this and the preceding two subsections on family life-related variables. We submit that we never will be able to understand what is going on until and unless we go beyond simple proxy variables like marital status or family size and get directly into the study of associated normative expectations. Such role expectations apparently vary with sex, age, employment status, region of the country, type of sport and recreational participation, country, length of marriage, age composition of the children in the family, and possibly other variables. To make things even more difficult, there are clearly interaction effects rather than simple linear, additive effects of these variables on such dependent variables as sport and recreational participation. It is high time some set of investigators begins to make some sense of all this through appropriately sophisticated data gathering and analysis strategies. Here again, we believe, the proposed Interdisciplinary Sequential Specificity Time Allocation Lifespan Model (see Smith & Macaulay, 1980; see also chapter one of this book) needs to be used as a research paradigm in order to make real headway. The bits and pieces of cross-sectional research on only a few of the total complex of variables involved are simply not adding up. We argue that they cannot add up and be properly synthesized because inappropriate research paradigms are being used, particularly in terms of ignoring longitudinal study, ignoring the full range of variables involved in the family life complex (notably, relevant role expectations), and ignoring the obvious presence of interaction effects of substantial importance. Other variables also need to be controlled statistically.

# Geographic Roles

Geographical context roles refer to the normative expectations for behavior that are associated with residential status in a particular building, block, neighborhood, community, city, state, region, or other geographical unit with social significance (but below the level of the whole nation; see the next subsection). In the earlier chapter dealing with social and historical context we reviewed a few of the many studies that examine the effects of such contextual variables as urban versus rural residence, placing particular emphasis on the opportunity structure aspects of those studies. We must now point out that it is quite possible that there are effects of geographical context roles on sport and recreational participation, in addition to contextual opportunity structure effects. Unfortunately, the research that has been done so far, to our knowledge, uniformly ignores direct measurement of normative expectations associated with geographical context roles as possible determinants of sport and outdoor recreational activity. All that one can find in the literature are crude proxy variables such as self-reported current or prior residence in one or another kind of geographical context. Here, too, there is clear need for much more research if the contextual effects are to be separated adequately from possible normative expectation or role effects.

## Nationality

Nationality is a status variable that has also been pretty well neglected by researchers in the field of sport and outdoor recreation. This is not surprising, for in order to study nationality effects directly, cross-national comparative studies are necessary. It is one thing to point to culture variations in levels of sport and recreational participation as contextual effects, as we did earlier in this chapter. It is quite another matter to demonstrate with comparative studies of representative samples of individuals from different nations (and major subcultures or ethnic groups within them) that, controlling for other social status and role variables, there are effects of nationality status upon sport and recreational activities. In principle something like this might be done with some of the data from the Szalai et al. (1972) 12-nation time budget study, though we are aware of no such analysis.

# CHAPTER FOUR

# Socioeconomic Status
# and Coparticipant Status Variables

In this chapter we continue the discussion of social position and role factors with a look at socioeconomic and coparticipant status factors.

## Socioeconomic Status

### Educational Status

The combination of role expectations as well as information and skills residue (and perhaps effects on personality dispositions, attitudinal dispositions, and intellectual capacities) that accompanies formal education (see Feldman & Newcomb, 1969) constitutes one of the most powerful variable complexes in social and behavioral science. This is not surprising because virtually all human behavior, particularly social behavior, is learned, and formal schools are major learning sites. Although it is not clear from prior research which of the foregoing aspects of education is responsible and to what degree, it is quite clear that higher levels of formal education are generally associated with greater participation in sport and outdoor recreation. This finding holds up with striking consistency in special purposive samples (Cheek, 1971a; Etzkorn, 1964; Hall, 1973; Jubenville, 1971; McIntyre, 1959; Torbert & Rogers, 1973), as well as in random samples of towns, cities, and states or provinces, both in the U.S. (Christensen & Yoesting, 1973; Kenyon, 1966; McKechnie, 1974; Reich, 1965; Snyder & Spreitzer, 1974) and in other countries (Heinila, 1959; Mihovilovic, 1973; Strzeminska, 1972; Wippler, 1968). There are minor exceptions only. Hendricks (1971) failed to find an effect of education on outdoor recreation in his urban sample but did find a weak relationship with urban leisure activities. Bultena and Wood (1970), in an upper income and highly educated sample of retirement community residents, found a zero-order relationship of education with active recreational participation, including sport, but this relationship vanished in a multivariate analysis (where only health and age, of the variables included, were important). Clearly, the latter is a special case. And Christensen and Yoesting (1973, 1976) found education lost explanatory power in multivariate analysis. However, Wippler (1968), in his multivariate analysis of data on a random sample of adults from Groningen, Netherlands, found education to be independently related to his dynamic-expansive leisure factor (described earlier) but weakly related to passive (vs. active) leisure pursuits and unrelated to outdoor (vs. indoor) leisure activities.

There are several national sample surveys over the past 3 decades that generally support the conclusion noted earlier—higher formal education is associated with greater sport and outdoor recreational participation. Some of these national surveys present only zero-order, uncontrolled relationships that confirm the conclusion. For the U.S., DeGrazia (1962) reports higher education to be associated with higher sport participation, more pleasure driving, and more frequent sport event attendance, but gardening and yard work were unrelated to education (as with age). A 1948 national survey reported by Sutton-Smith et al. (1963) showed education to be positively associated with active sport participation, watching sport events, and listening to sport on the radio. Robinson (1977) reports on a national U.S. urban sample that there is no general relationship between education and sport or outdoor recreation. However, he does find higher education to be related to greater active sport participation among employed people, while higher education is related to less active sport participation for not-employed females in the U.S. Both ORRRC studies in the early 1960s in the U.S. (Cicchetti, 1972; ORRRC, 1962a, b) support the generalization of higher education correlating with higher outdoor recreation participation, usually in multivariate analyses as well as in zero-order correlations or tables (see ORRRC, 1962b). The Miller Lite Survey (1983) also shows a positive correlation between education and sport participation, although one exception to the patterns is a higher percentage of nonparticipants among high school graduates than those with some high school. Kuhl et al. (1966) for Denmark, Fasting (1979) and the Norwegian Confederation of Sport (1984) for Norway, and White (1975), Curtis and Milton (1976), Statistics Canada (1978), and the Canada Fitness Survey (1983) for Canada report similar national sample survey results showing increased participation with greater education. The studies by Fasting, White, and Curtis and Milton all included multivariate analyses and in each case the relationship between education and participation held up in the analysis.

Finally, Robinson (1967) reports on the education effect upon sport participation for 10 nations' data from the Szalai et al. (1972) multinational time use study. He finds the same general trend as do the other studies but with some exceptions. In some countries there is a peak in active sport participation among those with some college education. And for one nation (a six-city French sample), the less educated participated more in active sport. For women who are employed there is a tendency for active sport participation to peak in the middle range of education level (some college), and for not-employed women there is a similar peak but some bimodality of the education distribution in terms of time devoted to active sports (mainly due to samples from Russia and West Germany). Because of the small amounts of time (in average minutes per day) involved in the latter data, however, these results are not particularly reliable, and the general trend of an association of higher education with higher active sport participation is the most proper cross-cultural conclusion to reach, as Robinson notes. Nevertheless, the inconsistencies observed bear further inquiry, especially into the meaning of having a certain level of education (that is, educational level role expectations) in different countries. As mentioned at the outset, we simply do not know what aspects or consequences of higher educational status are responsible for the observed correlation with higher sport and outdoor recreational participation.

## Social Class

Social class or social stratum role has been the subject of a good deal of research in the field of leisure and recreational activities. Most frequently it is studied in terms of its component variables or assumed determinants in modern and postindustrial societies, namely, educational level, occupational prestige level, and income. However, there are some studies that focus on social class or status more broadly, using

some kind of combined index of the foregoing variables or even directly
determining individual or family social reputation (rarely). As Kaplan
(1960), Luschen (1969), and others have pointed out, leisure and specifically sport and recreational participation are in part organized in society
along class or social status (social prestige level) lines. There are two
main aspects to the relationship of social status or class to sport and
outdoor recreational participation: (a) variations in the modal status
of participants in a particular activity and (b) variations in degree and
breadth of participation by individuals according to status. On the first
point, it has been shown in the U.S. and elsewhere that most sport
and outdoor recreational activities are to some extent class linked, in
the sense that disproportionate numbers of persons from one or more
social strata participate in them. For example, Stone examined status
differences in designations of "favorite" sports among 562 Minneapolis
residents in 1957, and Stone and Anderson replicated the study among
397 respondents in that city in 1975. The results of the two studies are
presented and compared in Anderson and Stone (1979). In the earlier
period there was considerable differentiation. Golf and tennis were
mentioned most often by high-status persons and thus designated as
high-status sports, while football, basketball, and swimming were
middle-class sports and baseball, boxing, and bowling were lower-class
sports. Fishing and hunting were not differentiated by strata. By 1975,
the number of sports that were class differentiated had declined. Golf
and tennis remained upper-class sports and were joined by skiing
(which was not among the sports mentioned in 1957). Bowling remained a lower-class sport. Strata differences in other sports were no
longer significant, indicating that there has been a process of homogeni-
zation. Anderson and Stone interpret the differences as indicating that
there has been democratization in sports that are spectator oriented,
while considerably greater differentiation remains among participatory
sports. Alternatively, with a Kansas City sample of middle-aged and
older people, Havighurst (1961) found higher status persons to engage
more in sport and flower gardening, middle-status persons to engage
more in fishing, and lower status persons to engage more in vegetable
gardening as their favorite leisure activities (see also Donald &
Havighurst, 1959). The social status participation patterns by sport also
vary across countries somewhat, even among modern and postindustrial societies (see Engstrom, 1974; Luschen, 1967, 1969). Much
more research is needed before we shall know why the existing social
status differentials in participation exist for specific sport and recreational activities. To discover this it will be necessary, in part, to in-
quire directly of people in distinct social strata how they view specific
sport and recreational activities in relation to their social class roles and
the normative expectations of such roles.

As for the second aspect of the relationship between social status and sport and recreational participation, a clear generalization stands out from the literature: The higher the social class or status of the individual, in general, the higher the amount and variety of sport and outdoor recreational participation. Although there are sometimes exceptions to this generalization, particularly with studies that examine only a few sports or outdoor recreational activities (for instance, MacDonald, McGuire, & Havighurst, 1949, studying children's evening outdoor play; White, 1955, studying use of local parks and playgrounds), many studies have shown greater sport participation or greater outdoor recreation participation and physical activity associated with higher social class or status (Havighurst, 1961; Hendricks, 1971; Hodges, 1964; McKnelly, 1973; Stebbins, 1969), not only in the U.S. but elsewhere as well (Luschen, 1969; Martindale, 1971). Another kind of exception that occurs in some studies is that middle-class people may show the highest sport and outdoor recreational participation, with some decline among the highest class levels, which nevertheless exceed lower status participation (for instance, Havighurst & Feigenbaum, 1959, found the middle class to be more community centered in its recreation, including sport and outdoor recreational participation, while the lower or working class was more home centered). This curvilinearity may account for weak or even nonexistent relationships (zero or near zero) observed in correlational statistics in some studies of the social class and sport or outdoor recreational participation relationship (Witt, 1971). In other instances of weak or zero relationships, attenuation owing to relatively class-homogeneous samples may be the cause (Hendry & Douglass, 1975, studying college students).

## Occupational Status

Occupational (prestige) status is a very commonly studied component of the larger socioeconomic status complex of variables. Even more than for composite social class measures, occupational prestige level has been found to be positively associated with sport or outdoor recreational participation. This generalization has held for studies with purposive samples of various types (Etzkorn, 1964, for campers; Standlee & Popham, 1958, for schoolteachers' participation in individual and team sports as well as sport event attendance; Jubenville, 1971, for hiking party leaders; Hall, 1973, for a haphazard sample of English and some Canadian women's participation in sport; Willmott, 1971, for samples from two English manufacturing firms' employees' participation in leisure activities in general, but for physical recreation and active recreation in particular; and Heyman & Jeffers, 1964, for a volunteer sample of older people in a North Carolina city). The relationship has also been found in a variety of random samples of cities, counties, and states or their equivalent (Burdge, 1969; Clarke, 1956; Dowell, 1967; Hendricks, 1971; Lundberg, Komarovsky, & McInerny, 1969; McKechnie, 1974; McKnelly, 1973; Mihovilovic, 1973; Morris, Pasewark, & Schultz, 1972; Reich, 1965; Sessoms, 1963; Zurn, 1971). There are exceptions, however. Kenyon (1966) found no significant effect of occupational prestige on physical recreation in general but did find the expected positive association for vigorous physical recreation. Wippler (1968) and Christensen and Yoesting (1973, 1976) found zero-order relationships as expected, but these vanished when other socioeconomic status variables were controlled statistically in multivariate analyses. The analysis of Christensen and Yoesting (1976) is particularly interesting in suggesting that the apparent effect of occupational prestige on outdoor recreation facility use is in fact the result of the association of educational level with occupational prestige and to a lesser extent is the result of the association of income with such prestige. They found that controlling for income and education in a partial correlation with participation eliminated the apparently strong occupational prestige effect, while controlling for the latter did not eliminate either the income or education effect on participation. Similar detailed multivariate analysis is much needed in other research on sport and outdoor recreational participation, hopefully avoiding the pitfalls of stepwise multiple regression analysis pointed out by Crandall (1976). Very few studies in the U.S. or elsewhere find no effect of occupational prestige level on participation at the zero order of relationship, especially if curvilinearity is allowed for (that is, some decline at the highest prestige level—professionals and related). The study by Snyder and Spreitzer (1974) is one of the apparent exceptions, finding no significant correlation of occupational prestige level with behavioral involvement in sport. However, no allowance is made for curvilinearity in the occupational prestige relationship (no tables are presented with cross tabulations, only correlations), and the behavioral involvement index has only a small component of actual sport activity, with more components relating to spectatorship, talking about sport, reading about sport, and in particular reading sport magazines. Cheek (1971b) is another exception, finding no occupational prestige effect on local park use; but this is only a single outdoor recreation type and does not disprove the broader generalization about sport and outdoor recreation of various types. And where Heinila (1959) finds more physical exercise in the working class, "other sports" are still more frequent in the middle class of the Finnish town studied.

Support for the generalization is also found in several national sample surveys in the U.S. and elsewhere (Canada Fitness Survey,

1983; Cicchetti, 1972; Hobart, 1975; ORRRC, 1962a, b; Sillitoe, 1967, 1969; Sutton-Smith et al., 1963; Veal, 1982). The Danish national survey is the only exception at the zero-order level of relationship (Anderson et al., 1969), but the reversal is a weak one (only 10% difference between high and low status in terms of active participation), and the sample is one of sport club members, not the total Danish population. The latter fact might artifactually create a negative relationship between occupational prestige and active sport participation if more lower prestige persons joined sport clubs in proportion to their numbers in the total population. In any event, there are other indications that the apparent relationship of higher occupational prestige with greater sport and recreational participation is not what it seems. For instance, in the ORRRC (1962a) report, the zero-order effect of occupational prestige is much reduced when a multivariate analysis is performed, controlling other sociodemographic variables, though the occupational prestige effect remains significant for males (not for females). Part of the problem seems to be that craftspersons cluster with the managers and officials in their higher sport and outdoor recreation activity, while sales and clerical workers cluster with blue-collar workers in having lower activity; the professionals are also weak in their sport and recreational activity, other factors controlled. In analyzing Canadian national sample data, Hobart (1975) shows that the occupational prestige effect on sport participation is really significant only for women under 35 and men under 55, then becomes weak for higher ages. White (1975) goes further with the same data to show that the apparent zero-order effect of occupational prestige on sport and athletic participation vanishes when education and income are controlled in a multivariate analysis.

Thus it is quite possible that the widely prevalent observed zero-order association of occupational prestige with sport and outdoor recreational or athletic participation is in large part the indirect result of the association of both income and education with both occupational prestige and sport and recreational participation. To determine whether occupational prestige status exercises any independent effect, it will be necessary to determine in future research whether there are normative expectations associated with higher occupational prestige roles that affect sport and outdoor recreational participation. Such investigations will have to include measures of income, educational level, and social class statuses and their corresponding role expectations, and investigators will have to perform careful multivariate analyses, allowing for the possibilities of both curvilinearity and multicollinearity, as well as interaction effects.

The other aspect of occupational prestige that has been investigated in relation to sport and recreation is analogous to what has also been done for social class status. Several researchers have been concerned with the modal occupational prestige of the participants in particular sport or outdoor recreational activities. As would be expected, there are significant variations in the empirical patterns of occupational prestige from what would be expected on the basis of the societal occupational prestige distribution. Thus in an early study, Clarke (1956) found no occupational prestige association with hunting, bowling, gardening, or picnicking in his study of a random sample of Columbus, Ohio adults, but he found attending football games characteristic of occupational prestige level II (second highest), golf characteristic of level III, and fishing and zoo attendance characteristic of level V (the lowest level). More recently, Burdge (1969) found picnicking to be relatively common at all occupational prestige levels in his study of Allegheny County, Pennsylvania, while most other sport and recreational activities were characteristic of either the highest or second highest of his four prestige levels. In common with other studies, he found working in a flower garden, playing golf, sailing, winter sports, and tennis to be characteristic of the highest occupational prestige level; fishing, hunting, hiking, boating, bowling, and baseball characterized prestige level II. Very few sport or outdoor recreational activities characterized level III—work in a vegetable garden, softball, basketball, touch football, and attending stock car races or boxing matches (prestige level I attended most kinds of sport events most often). The lowest prestige level (IV) was characterized only by attendance at wrestling matches and having no hobbies, playing no sports, and attending no sport events. The national sample survey reported by Sutton-Smith et al. (1963) confirms that golf and tennis are characteristic of the highest occupational prestige persons, with professionals lagging somewhat behind other high-prestige occupations. Cunningham, Montoye, Metzner, and Keller (1970) present yet a different pattern (though golf still emerges as a top-prestige sport) in their study of a sample from the Tecumseh, Michigan area. Their study is noteworthy in showing how highly variable the occupational prestige patterns can be for different types of recreation when these are examined for different age groups. The chaos is so complete that one is again driven to the conclusion that only by inquiring about the meaning of different sport and recreational activities for persons of different ages and occupational prestige levels could we ever hope to understand the data they present. One interesting effort in this regard is presented by Anderson and Stone in the report of the Minneapolis studies discussed earlier (Anderson & Stone, 1979). Respondents to the 1957 and 1975 surveys were asked to identify the activities that come to mind when they hear the word "sport." Anderson and Stone viewed the responses to this question as an indication of the meanings associated with sport as a symbol and hence of the "saliency" of different activities as sport activities. Responses in the 1957 study indicated significant strata differences in the number of activities mentioned and in the saliency of particular sports. There were no significant differences in the number of sports mentioned in 1975 and fewer differences for particular sports. As in the findings for strata differences in favorite sport, those sports that were differentiated in 1960 but not in 1975 were mainly spectator-oriented: baseball, boxing, wrestling, and tennis (the latter increasingly a spectator sport in the 1970s). As well, two sports that were not strata-differentiated in 1957, hunting and fishing, were differentiated in 1975. The authors note, however, that the results may be a function of the fact that the number of respondents mentioning these activities in 1975 was small (less than 15% for each).

Bishop and Ikeda (1970) make some further headway in this direction by attempting to cluster analyze different leisure patterns. They are able to show three important dimensions in types of leisure activities—an occupational prestige-related highbrow versus lowbrow dimension, a masculinity-femininity dimension, and a dimension involving a high degree of mental or physical involvement in work and low degree of interpersonal orientation. Later on, in looking at work on values and attitudes related to leisure activities, we shall have occasion to examine other similar attempts to characterize activities along various dimensions that could help us understand the varying occupational prestige-related patterns that are observed.

## Resources and Access Factors

These social background variables of individuals are generally not well understood in social science research on discretionary social participation, but one might expect the situation to be better in the area of sport and outdoor recreational participation than elsewhere. Unfortunately, this is not the case. Instead of there being numerous studies using finely detailed measures of relevant sport and recreational resources and opportunities, such studies are very few in number and mainly confined to recreational travel research. The most common measure of resources and access factors in sport and outdoor recreation research, as for other kinds of social participation, is individual or family income—a crude proxy variable for various more specific measures of access and resources that should be used, in our opinion.

Nonetheless, the results are generally quite clear here: Higher individual or family income is usually associated with higher sport and outdoor recreational participation. This conclusion is supported for small or special purposive samples (Cheek, 1971a, for zoo-goers; Standlee & Popham, 1958, for spectator sport participants among

Indiana schoolteachers; Jubenville, 1971, for hiking party leaders; Vaux, 1975, for wilderness users; Bultena & Wood, 1970, for active retirement community residents), for samples of cities, counties, parts of states, or states using broader measures of sport or outdoor recreational activity (Christensen & Yoesting, 1973, 1976; Hobart, 1975; Kenyon, 1966; McKechnie, 1974; McKnelly, 1973; *Ontario Recreation Survey*, 1977; Physical Activity Patterns, 1981; Reich, 1965) in the U.S. and elsewhere (Mihovilovic, 1973; Wippler, 1968), and for national sample surveys with broad measures both from the U.S. (Cicchetti, 1972; DeGrazia, 1962; Miller Lite Report, 1983; ORRRC, 1962a, b; Robinson, 1977) and elsewhere (Norwegian Confederation of Sport, 1984; Statistics Canada, 1978; White, 1975).

The main exception to the income relationship is that the association tends to decline at the highest income levels; that is, once past upper middle-income levels, further income increments lead to less rather than to more sport or outdoor recreational participation. This can be most clearly seen in analyses that control for other social background factors such as education and occupational prestige, as well as age, sex, marital status, and so on (ORRRC, 1962b), and that use a multivariate analysis procedure such as multiple classification analysis or multiple analysis of variance. Sometimes this effect shows up directly as greater participation for upper middle-income persons in a cross tabulation (Reich, 1965). There are variations in the relationship by age (income not important for people under 35 years of age—Hobart, 1975), by gender and employment status (income negatively related to sport or outdoor recreation for unemployed females—Robinson, 1977), and by type of activity involved (little or no effect of income upon cycling, fishing, hunting, or walking for pleasure—ORRRC, 1962a).

The latter findings, in particular, suggest that income is a proxy for resources and access opportunities. Those kinds of sport and outdoor recreational activities that involve the least expenditure for travel or equipment are less likely to show income effects. Unfortunately, we know of no studies that systematically examine income effects upon different types of sport and recreational activity controlling for other social background variables, though this could be done with existing national survey data. Studies where income shows no zero-order relationship with sport or outdoor recreational participation are rare, though the effect may vanish when other socioeconomic status variables like education or occupational prestige are controlled statistically in multivariate analyses (Wippler, 1968). The effect of income is likely to be weak, of course, where the sport or recreational activity involved is one that requires little or no travel or equipment and where the sample is narrow in its income range. Also, income may show no relationship to sport or recreational activity when the specific dependent variable is one (for instance, visiting a nearby national forest) that presents a local sample with little or no differential access problems (Lindsay & Ogle, 1972).

As we noted earlier, there has been relatively little sport and outdoor recreation research that examines resources and opportunities in much more detail, with the exception being studies of recreational travel, usually by economists. There are quite a few studies of the latter type, all of them showing that the number of recreational travel trips from a given site (for instance, county or metropolitan area) to a given outdoor recreational site elsewhere (for instance, a national or state forest or park, or a commercial outdoor recreation area) is powerfully affected by the distance between the two sites (Beaman, 1974, 1976; Cesario, 1975; Freund & Wilson, 1974; O'Rourke, 1974). In all of these studies, distance is used as a proxy variable for travel costs or trip costs, and there tends to be an effect of distance that generally increases as a power of the distance, not linearly. Thus, nearer sites are much more favored, other things equal, over more distant ones. However, for very short distances (20-60 miles), the distance does not matter much, and for very long distances the effect of additional miles decreases rather than increases (see Beaman, 1974, 1976; Wilkinson, 1973; Wolfe, 1972).

Very few studies actually measure trip costs directly. When Keith and Workman (1975) did so for fishermen using a stretch of stream in the U.S. Northwest, they found significant effects of both transportation and on-site costs of users as well as opportunity costs (in the sense of foregone income for weekday fishing). The latter study is striking because it shows only mixed relationships for individual annual income with use, while the more refined measures of trip costs are very consistently significant predictors (lower trip costs of all sorts being associated with greater use of the particular fishing area by men from various counties of origin).

There are some studies that examine the effects of car ownership upon recreational or sport participation, with mixed results. Unfortunately, very few studies control simultaneously for income and other social background variables, so that even where car ownership seems to have significant effects (see O'Rourke, 1974, for various studies cited) it is unclear whether this is a socioeconomic status effect or a resources and access effect. A rare exception, then, is Robinson's (1977) multivariate analysis of an urban U.S. national sample showing that auto access was significantly and positively associated with active sport participation but not with outdoor recreation, with other variables (including income and socioeconomic status factors like education) controlled. The lack of an income effect on outdoor recreation other than outdoor active sport may result from the importance of garden and yard work, walking for pleasure, and other low-resource activities in this dependent variable once active sport has been removed.

More commonly, possession of an automobile is positively associated with recreational travel (O'Rourke, 1974), but one cannot say whether this is an income effect in general, a perceptual or psychological effect, or an access effect, owing to inadequate methodology and statistical analysis. Sometimes car ownership is unrelated to sport or outdoor recreational activity (Witt, 1971), just as sometimes annual income is irrelevant for very short travel distances to a given recreation site (Lindsay & Ogle, 1972). As Harry (1972) suggests, income is likely to have a permissive effect on sport and outdoor recreational activity, accounting for the lack of importance of additional income above upper middle-income levels noted earlier. Similarly, where car ownership is very widespread one would expect little or no effect on sport and outdoor recreational participation, while much greater effects would be expected when car ownership or other access is less widespread but not very low. More detailed study is needed here, for studies like that of LaPage and Ragain (1974) make it clear that recreational vehicles make important differences in how people use the outdoors for recreation.

The study just referred to is particularly interesting in suggesting the range of resource and opportunity factors that need to be studied for all kinds of sport and outdoor recreation but that have *not* been studied. LaPage and Ragain (1974) report data from an 8-year panel study of camping families recruited at several large campgrounds in the U.S. Northeast. They find that a decline in camping is associated with, among other factors, purchase of a seasonal home—a clearly important resource whose importance has not been systematically examined for sport and outdoor recreation. Increased camping was found to be associated with such resource or access factors as tent camping giving way to recreational vehicle camping ("campers" or "travel trailers" or even "motor homes") and with weekend trips giving way to the rental of a camping site for the entire season. Another study of camping and recreational vehicle use by Born (1976a) employed discriminant function analysis to identify variables that distinguish four subgroups of recreational vehicle owners. The subgroups consisted of users of (a) private urban trailer parks, (b) private rural trailer parks, (c) developed public land campgrounds, and (d) undeveloped or partially developed campgrounds. The transition represents a shift from a more to less comfortable living style. Analysis of 21 variables identified 6 that were important discriminators, and of these, financial factors figured prominently. Two of the six, income and value of equipment, are direct financial indicators. Other discriminators were educational level of the male member of the couple, a proxy measure for income, and percentage of the year lived in a recreational vehicle, which was negatively associated with ownership of a permanent conventional home and thus is another indirect measure of income. (The other two discriminating variables were noneconomic characteristics of the woman, specifically her amount of preretirement camping experience and her age.)

Clearly this kind of work needs to be done more frequently, for it is not enough to know annual or monthly income, nor even that possession of leisure resources increases with higher socioeconomic status (Thomas, 1956). And what is one to make of the finding of Hendricks (1971) that home dwellers (as contrasted with apartment dwellers) are more involved in outdoor natural recreation while less involved in urban recreational activities, controlling distance and socioeconomic status? Clearly, life-style effects need to be considered, and status or role factors need to be separated from both resource-access factors and from motivational and information factors. Finally, there are a few studies that indicate the importance of resources other than physical property. Angrist (1967) thus shows that there is more leisure activity for middle-class, female college graduate women with children if they have significant household paid help and child care. And Robinson (1977) shows with his national urban U.S. sample that household help is associated with less active sport participation for employed men and unemployed (not in the labor force included) women but is significantly associated with more active sport participation among employed women, in a multivariate analysis controlling other social background variables, including income and education. (Robinson also shows that possession of a TV set is very strongly associated with amount of TV viewing in this same multivariate analysis. Here the possession of a TV set is not so much a permissive factor as an indication of preferences, in all likelihood, because most homes in the U.S. had TV sets at the time of data collection, and lack of one might indicate dislike of TV, more than anything else.)

## Occupational Role

Type of occupational role is a very different perspective on the effects of occupation on sport and recreational participation. Corresponding to the earlier concept of occupational "situs" as contrasted with occupational "status" (prestige), occupational-type inquiries in the study of sport and recreation have grown up in the past 20 years out of a dissatisfaction with overemphasis on the prestige dimension of work. Gerstl (1961) was perhaps the first to make the point strongly for the study of leisure. He compared the activities of professors, dentists, and advertising professionals and managers, all of roughly comparable high occupational prestige, finding advertising professionals and managers and dentists to be more involved in sport participation than professors. Similarly, Jordan (1963) found more active and passive sport participation among attorneys and physicists than among sociologists. Drawing on Dubin's (1956) demonstration that work is not a central life interest of most industrial workers, and upon Kaplan's (1960) discussion of work and leisure, a dozen or more studies have been done in the past 20 years attempting to understand how one's type of work and the characteristics of one's work are related to one's leisure participation, with several books devoted to the general topic in recent years (Clayre, 1974; Parker, 1971; Salaman, 1974; Torbert & Rogers, 1973).

The general analytical argument has boiled down to three basic positions: a compensatory thesis, that people seek in their recreation what they lack in their jobs (see Burch, 1969; Knopp, 1972; Noe, 1971, who reviews several prior studies); a spillover thesis, that people seek in their recreation situations that are similar to their work situations and activities (see Meissner, 1971; Parker, 1971; Torbert & Rogers, 1973; Wippler, 1968); and an independence thesis, that what people seek in their recreation has no relation to the nature of their job (see Bacon, 1975). These three perspectives have been labeled in various ways by different researchers, and there have been useful attempts to explicate the underlying dimensions of differences among them by Kando and Summers (1971), Kelly (1972), Parker (1971), Shepard (1974), and others. The latter author views the question of work-leisure relationships in terms of a larger philosophical and analytic context: He views the spillover ("extension") thesis as integral to a holistic view of the individual and society, while the compensatory ("opposition") and independence ("neutrality") theses are two variations on the more general theme of segmentalism, a view that there are different and separated institutions in society and differentiated spheres of an individual's life. Though White (1975) concludes a brief review of the literature agreeing with the spillover hypothesis, and Torbert and Rogers' (1973) book is quite convincing on the same side of the argument, much more research will be needed from national samples in different countries before we can be very confident about which of the theses is more nearly correct and under what conditions. The appropriate conclusion for the present seems to be that one's occupation and working conditions at times have a significant effect on one's recreational choices, and when there is such an effect, there is more likely to be spillover than compensation. However, none of the studies cited except Wippler's (1968) have performed multivariate analyses in trying to understand work-leisure relationships, so that all of the previous work except Wippler's might look quite different with other socio-demographic variables controlled. Wippler himself concluded that the connection between work and leisure, while present, was probably weaker than most of the researchers investigating it would like to accept. This argues for the independence thesis, with only weak spill-over effects, a conclusion future research of a similarly sophisticated nature will have to confirm or disconfirm (note, however, that Wippler used stepwise regression analysis, which probably distorted some of his multivariate results and conclusions based thereon).

## Coparticipant Status

Coparticipant status and role expectations have received very little attention either theoretically or empirically by those concerned with sport and recreational participation. Meyersohn (1969), in an overview of leisure research, commented that little attempt had been made to study the groups in which leisure takes place, with most studies with random samples carefully eliminating the natural connectedness of individuals. Burch (1969), in a study of camping behavior, came to the conclusion that a "personal community" explanation was crucial to understanding why some people participate in camping, or a certain kind of camping, and others do not. More explicitly, this meant relating present camping behavior of individuals to the camping behavior of their parents and spouses. The work that was reviewed earlier under the heading of life cycle stage and family role constellation can be fit in here also, in some cases. Willmott's (1971) study of manufacturing firm employees showed that the majority of out-of-home leisure and recreation took place with one or more family members, spouse or children. A similar pattern was obtained by Dynes (1977), whose survey of registrants at a seashore campsite indicated that in both at-home and out-of-home leisure activities fathers most often participated with one or more family members, rather than alone or with nonfamilial coparticipants.

Further evidence of the importance of family members as co-participants in leisure activities is found in studies by Orthner (1975, 1976) and Kelly (1978). Orthner's work showed that joint recreational activities with one's spouse were a significant part of total leisure, though varying with the stage of the marriage; Kelly found that family members are the most frequent coparticipants in the leisure activities of adults in three communities: a Western university town, a Midwest mill town, and an Eastern new (planned) town. An analysis of the breakdown of activities by life cycle was conducted for the Eastern new town, again showing differences in activities related to marriage and parenthood. Among the married and childless, spouses are the most frequent leisure companions, while those with children most often engage in leisure activities with children and spouse.

In another place, it was noted that middle-class people are more likely to have community-centered leisure styles while lower status individuals are more likely to have family-centered styles, again referring to the matter of with whom one engages in one's leisure and recreational behavior (Havighurst & Feigenbaum, 1959). Cheek (1971b) has addressed this general topic most directly in developing the beginnings of a "theory of not-work." He shows, with national sample data from the U.S., that males generally go to work alone but go to a local park with others: The reversal in proportions is on the order of 75-25% to 25-75%. In asking further about male participation in recreational activities, he finds that people also tend very markedly to attend movies, go to sport events, visit friends, go to church, and go to nightclubs or bars with others (invariably upward of 70% of the time).

A number of other studies also support the conclusion that sport and outdoor recreational activity tend to be engaged in with friends or relatives, even when the nature of the activity would in theory permit one to engage in it alone or merely with strangers. Lee (1972) refers to this as the "social definition of outdoor recreation places" (p. 68). For instance, Yancey and Snell (1971) found that almost every leisure and recreational activity they investigated, for a sample of middle and lower status people in a Tennessee city, involved informal groups of family and friends. Field (1971), studying a variety of outdoor recreation settings, found that participation of an individual with others predominated (at 90% or greater), except for neighborhood play of youth. Connor, Johannis, and Walters (1955) found in their small sample of high school students and their parents that both types of respondents stated that they did some or many things with each other as recreational activities. Wade (1973), in a slightly different type of study, found that interpersonal discussion was associated with leisure activities, including sport and outdoor recreation. Other strands of evidence come from studies like those of Etzkorn (1964), who found sociability (interpersonal contact) to be a key motivation for camping, and Lundberg et al. (1969), who found both high school youth and adults tended to define having a "good time" in terms of sport or outings with friends or relatives. Studies using better samples, whether of parts of states (Christensen & Yoesting, 1973, 1976; Field & O'Leary, 1973; O'Leary, Field, & Schreuder, 1974), national samples (Wonneberger, 1968, for the German Democratic Republic; Anderson et al., 1969, for Denmark), or cross-national comparative samples (Ferge et al., 1972), show essentially the same kinds of results (see also the literature review by O'Rourke, 1974).

The Ferge et al. (1972) data from the 12-nation Szalai et al. (1972) time budget study are perhaps most convincing. For leisure activities (including sport and outdoor recreation but not mass media use) in general, 10 of 12 nations studied indicated that 80-90% of leisure activities are done with other persons, usually friends and family (the German Democratic Republic and the Bulgaria data were the exceptions, with only 40-60% of leisure activities spent with others). Further, both Christensen and Yoesting (1973, 1976) and Field and O'Leary (1973) have shown that the effects observed hold up when multivariate analyses are performed. Indeed, the latter study showed that coparticipation with friends or family in four outdoor recreational activities was generally a much better predictor than the usual sociodemographic variables (except for fishing). The total variance explained jumped from under 5% to 20-30% for powerboating, swimming, and visiting a beach when coparticipation as a variable was added to the set of predictors like age, gender, and so on. Moreover, different types of outdoor recreation have different coparticipation "profiles," so to speak. Coparticipants are more likely to be family members for swimming and visiting a beach, whereas they are more likely to be friends for fishing and powerboating (or combinations of friends and family).

Bell and Healey (1973) have offered a theoretical explanation for variations in the extent to which spouses participate in leisure together. They argue that coparticipation is characteristic of the modern or nontraditional family, where there is far less gender role segregation than in the traditional family. Thus joint leisure activity by husband and wife is seen as an extension of a more general diminution of gender-segregated activities (see also Komarovsky, 1967; Scheuch, 1960). Salaman (1974) offers a different kind of explanation for coparticipation with fellow workers. Studying two different kinds of "occupational communities," those of architects and railway workers, he suggests that people whose occupations place them in an occupational community (with generally close interpersonal ties to coworkers and a sense of in-group occupational identification) are more likely to participate in leisure activities with coworkers than people in other kinds of occupations. The most basic explanation for the importance of coparticipant status as a factor in sport and outdoor recreational activities is simply that such activities are generally viewed as a kind of enjoyment, and for human beings enjoyment is usually enhanced by coparticipation with family or friends.

Finally, membership status in sport or outdoor recreational voluntary groups has been virtually unstudied as an explanatory factor affecting either formally organized or informal sport and recreational participation. To most, perhaps, it seems too "obvious" or "trivial" as a variable. Yet we would argue that it is potentially important. It is unclear, for instance, whether being a member of such a formal group actually enhances the likelihood of informal sport and recreational activity of the same (or different) types as those that are part of the group's focus and purpose. Such a spillover or generalization effect is quite possible, but we know of no studies of the issue (though Hobart, 1975, shows voluntary organization membership in general to relate to recreational activity). Moreover, it is not even clear whether membership status in such a group is a cause or effect (or both) of active sport and outdoor recreational participation. Clearly some research on such matters is needed.

# CHAPTER FIVE

# Experiences and Activities

The literature on socialization into sport and recreational activities has been expanding in recent years, and several quite comprehensive reviews and critiques have appeared (e.g., Coakley, 1981, 1986; Greendorfer, 1978; Iso-Ahola, 1980; Kelly, 1980; McPherson, 1980, 1986). This chapter presents some of the major findings of the research to date and indicates a few aspects of theory and needed research that are considered important. First it should be pointed out that not all prior activities and experiences can be considered part of the socialization process. Socialization includes strictly only those prior experiences and activities that are part of the process of shaping a member of society and inculcating the norms for behavior in various situations and roles. There are many other nonnormatively related experiences, often quite idiosyncratic, that may affect social participation including sport and recreational participation (for instance, a chance encounter with an athletic star that makes a big impression on a youth or a serious accident that occurs during a person's early recreational activity).

## Experience and Activities Studies

Many studies confirm that childhood participation in sport and outdoor recreational activity is associated with later adult participation of a similar sort (Bevins, Bond, Corcoran, McIntosh, & McNeil, 1968; Burch & Wenger, 1967; Buse & Enosh, 1977; Christensen, 1972; Christensen & Yoesting, 1973, 1976; Hall, 1976; Hendee, Catton, Marlow, & Brockman, 1968; Hendry & Douglas, 1975; Kelly, 1977, 1978; Laakso, 1978, 1980; McPherson, 1978a; ORRRC, 1962a, c; Snyder & Spreitzer, 1976; Sofranko & Nolan, 1972). However, very little research has been done relating type of child-rearing practices of parents to the types of sport and recreational activities engaged in by their children either when young or older. Roberts and Sutton-Smith (1962) are one exception, showing that achievement training is related to the choice of games of physical skill (sport), that obedience training is related to the choice of games of strategy, and that responsibility training is related to the choice of games of chance, both cross-culturally and for schoolchildren in the United States.

Childhood participation in sport and outdoor recreation, in turn, seems clearly related to one's parents' participation in or encouragement of participation in sport and outdoor recreation, for the source of introduction to such activities is most frequently the family (Greendorfer, 1978; Greendorfer & Lewko, 1978; Kenyon & McPherson, 1973; Koehler, 1973; Orlick, 1974; ORRRC, 1962a; Pudelkiewicz, 1970; Sofranko & Nolan, 1972). Moreover, it is clear that sport and recreational participation by high school or college youth (Butcher, 1983; Dowell, 1973; Koehler, 1973; Larson & Spreitzer, 1974; Moore, 1969; Smith, 1979; Snyder & Spreitzer, 1978; Stebbins, 1969) and by adults (Kenyon & McPherson, 1973; ORRRC, 1962a; Snyder & Spreitzer, 1973) is related to parental participation or encouragement in such activities. Additionally, research has indicated the importance of school personnel (Kenyon & McPherson, 1973) and peers as socializing agents (Greendorfer, 1978; Kenyon & McPherson, 1973), although in general these agents have been shown to be less important than the family. Quite another direction of research is the evidence that higher socioeconomic status and education of one's parents is associated with greater sport and recreational participation of the individual (Hall, 1973; Hobart, 1975; McIntyre, 1959; Rehberg & Cohen, 1976; Stebbins, 1969).

The many studies cited above showing the correspondence between sport and recreational activities engaged in during childhood and throughout the life cycle have been taken as evidence of the stability of these behaviors. Iso-Ahola (1980) has recently argued that recreational involvement is best viewed as dialectical, involving both stability and change. The evidence for this is taken from several studies. First, research by Yoesting and Burkhead (1973) shows that leisure patterns change over the life cycle and that during particular periods some activities are initiated while others are dropped. Related research by Kelly (1974, 1977) indicates that leisure activities engaged in by adults are nearly equally divided between those begun during childhood and those begun in adulthood. The final source of support for the dialectical view is taken from data provided by Christensen and Yoesting (1977) on the substitutability of recreational activities. Their finding that 60% of 300 survey respondents say that they could replace their current recreational activities with other activities with similar satisfaction "implies that there is cognitive and behavioral flexibility in leisure participation" (Iso-Ahola, 1980, p. 141).

An example of the few lines of research on prior experiences that fall outside the category of socialization, strictly defined, is the research on success or satisfactoriness of prior sport and recreational participation. Orlick (1974), for instance, indicates that his study of young children showed their sport activity was directly affected by the child's expectancies for satisfaction or dissatisfaction in such activity, which in turn were directly affected by prior positive or negative experiences in such activity. In interviews with dropouts from a boys' soccer program in Halifax, Pooley (1981) found that one third stated that they left because the competitive element was stressed too much. Ward, Hardman, and Almond (n.d.), Heinila (1964), and Fisher and Driscoll (1975) indicate similar results for youth. The work of these and other authors, and especially that of Orlick and his colleagues (Orlick, 1973, 1974, 1980; Orlick & Botterill, 1979), have contributed to a mounting literature on the evils of excessive competition and organization of children's sport. There has been less attention to adult nonparticipation and dropouts. One exception is the work of Boothby, Tungatt, and Townsend (1981). In lengthy interviews with 250 adults in an English suburban community, these authors found that the most frequently cited reason for ceasing participation in sport activity was "loss of interest." Other reasons included lack of facilities, declining fitness, and physical disability. Concerns with program orientation and emphasis were notably absent from the factors cited by the respondents.

In a treatment of the effects of early experiences and activities more generally, the review of literature reported by Loy, Birrell, and Rose (1976) indicates that orientations toward sport are a function of sex, level of participation, and context of participation. Specifically, males and those involved in more highly organized and competitive contests display more professionalized orientations toward play, favoring winning and skill development over fairness and equity in game playing. More recent research reported by Theberge, Curtis, and Brown (1982) has further explicated the nature of this relationship. These authors again found that orientations toward playing games are a function of sex and level of participation. In particular, cross-national data from five countries show that elite athletes (members of the national team in track and field) held more professionalized orientations than adult members of the general population in these countries. Interestingly, there was little evidence of sex differences among the elite athletes. There were, however, sex differences among adult and adolescent samples of the general population from English Canada and French Canada, confirming previously reported findings of sex differences in orientations toward games. An additional finding of the Theberge et al. (1982) study is that among members of the general populations of adults and adolescents in English Canada and French Canada, orientations were not significantly related to a variety of sport involvement measures (e.g., present sport involvement and parental encouragement for sport participation). As a result, multivariate controls for sport involvement did not significantly affect the association between orientations and sex. This finding suggests that while differences in experiences and activities are related to orientations, it is not yet clear what aspects or features of these experiences account for the association.

Still a different approach to the impact of prior experiences and activities on sport and outdoor recreational participation is illustrated by Mercer (1971b) in his review of the literature regarding the effects of perception on travel to rural outdoor recreation sites. He points out that the "awareness space" of the individual is crucial in determining how one makes an outdoor recreation travel and participation decision. This awareness space is clearly a direct residue of prior experiences, whether firsthand or mediated, with particular recreation sites. As Aldskogius (1967) points out, the relevant portion of the environment for individual decision making is only the unique action space of the individual—a mental map of spatial variations in expected recreational utilities (satisfactions). The powerful importance of awareness space is shown empirically in only a few studies, such as that of Lime (1969), who showed that 80% of his sample of auto campers coming to a national forest in Minnesota had decided on their camping site prior to leaving home, generally based on prior personal experience or mediated experience of the site involved (see also Born, 1976a, b). Sonnenfeld (1966), in a related study, notes that it is important to distinguish natives and nonnatives of a particular area in attempting to understand outdoor recreational travel behavior. Nonnatives of an area are likely to have had more varied travel experience and hence be more discriminating in their choice of recreational sites, whereas area natives, lacking this varied experience, will tend to be less discriminating. Of course, it would be good to measure degree of variation in individual travel experience directly rather than by the proxy variable of native versus nonnative status.

While the increasing interest in socialization into sport and recreational activities in recent years has contributed a body of information about this process, much of this work is plagued by methodological and conceptual problems (see Coakley, 1986). The first of these problems is that most of the research has been conducted among participants. (For an exception, see Greendorfer, 1979.) Without adequate comparative analysis of participants and nonparticipants, the usefulness of this work in explaining both initial involvement and continued participation is limited.

Another sampling problem is that for the most part research has been conducted among white males participating in the more organized and institutionalized forms of sport and recreation. The sex bias of this work has recently been corrected in some measure by the works of Greendorfer (1977, 1978, 1979), Snyder and Spreitzer (1976, 1978), Smith (1979), and Butcher (1983). Their research indicates that we should be wary of assumptions of similarity in the socialization processes of males and females, especially in their socialization into sport. One pattern suggested by the literature is that "there appears to be a need for a greater number and variety of significant others for females as opposed to males, if they are to continue being involved into the high school and college years" (McPherson, 1980, p. 256).

Other limitations of the work to date are that only a couple of the studies cited in this chapter are longitudinal in nature and only a couple are of large representative samples of a state, province, or nation. The use of multivariate statistical analysis controlling for a variety of extraneous but potentially powerful variables is infrequent as well. There are theoretical models beginning to be used to guide more sophisticated research and analyses, however (Kenyon & McPherson, 1973; Orlick, 1974; Sofranko & Nolan, 1972), so that future research in this area should improve over time in the next several years. It is high time that this happened, given the demonstrably important role in affecting sport and outdoor recreational participation that the present category of variables has, even based on the fragmentary and inadequate evidence so far available.

## The General Activity Pattern

There is another aspect of experiences and activities in addition to the foregoing learning and socialization aspect, namely, the co-variation of sport and outdoor recreational activities with each other and with other kinds of social activities that the individual engages in during the same general time period (for instance, in the same month or year). In the introductory chapter to Smith and Macaulay (1980), such covariation is referred to as the General Activity Pattern. Now, in the present volume, let us examine some evidence from sport and outdoor recreation research supporting or otherwise bearing on that pattern. First, there are indirect kinds of evidence of the pattern in the covariation of explanatory variables for sport and outdoor recreation participation along with other kinds of discretionary participation. Although this kind of evidence will be reviewed more generally in the concluding chapter, it should be noted here that there is much evidence of such covariation in the sport and outdoor recreation literature. For instance, Burdge (1969) finds that people higher in education and socioeconomic status participate more in various leisure activity types, including outdoor recreation, urban recreation (golf, movies, concerts, walks, pleasure driving), sport, attending sport events, and hobbies, based on his sample of a Pennsylvania county including Philadelphia. Or in the motivational realm, Kenyon (1968) finds that six different domains of leisure attitudes for which he developed indices are all positively intercorrelated and generally at statistically significant levels.

There is also, however, a variety of direct evidence bearing on the relationship of sport or outdoor recreational activities to each other and to other kinds of discretionary social participation. In the leisure and recreation literature, some attention has been given to aspects of the General Activity Pattern under the term "substitutability." Hendee and Burdge (1974) define leisure activity substitutability as "interchangeability of recreational activities in satisfying participants' motives, needs, and preferences" (p. 157). They see this notion as originating in conceptual and empirical typologies of leisure and recreational activities that refer to common meanings and consequences (satisfactions) of different activities (see Bishop, 1970; Christensen & Yoesting, 1977; Field, 1971; Hendee, Gale, & Catton, 1971; Moss & Lamphear, 1970; Yoesting & Burkhead, 1973). In particular, they suggest that common social (coparticipant) and personality variables may cause such substitutability. At the very least, outdoor recreational activities are substitutable (that is, covary or are associated) because they occur in the same factor when a factor analysis of a variety of types of leisure and recreational activity types is performed on a sample of a Pennsylvania county (see Burdge, 1969, for the data factor analyzed). Within such factor clusters, activities may be substitutable with little loss of satisfaction, they argue. Failure of most studies to take account of this covariation, especially when investigating outdoor recreation demand and doing planning based on such studies, is deplored.

Other empirical studies find clear evidence of the covariation of outdoor recreation and sport activities among themselves for various kinds of samples (see Heinila, 1959; McKechnie, 1974; Ritchie, 1975), including a U.S. national sample (Proctor, 1962). The latter study is particularly convincing, for it is one of the extremely rare studies of outdoor recreation that reports the results of a principal components factor analysis prior to some kind of (usually orthogonal) rotation. Here we see that there are all positive correlations in a matrix of 15 outdoor recreational activities and that there is a very large first principal components factor extracted on which all 15 activities have positive loadings of 0.30 or more, with the second factor being much smaller in size. This is clear evidence of a general factor underlying outdoor recreation participation, and the fact that a Varimax rotation of the principal components solution yields four meaningful factors does nothing to vitiate this conclusion (drawn by us, not Proctor).

No other study we are aware of reports such principal components factor analysis results, though there are several studies that report rotated Varimax factors extracted either for leisure and recreation activities generally or for outdoor recreation specifically (Bishop, 1970; McKechnie, 1974; Ritchie, 1975; Schmitz-Scherzer, Rudinger, Angleitner, & Bierhoff-Alfermann, 1974). This failure makes it impossible to tell whether such studies confirm or disconfirm Proctor's results. At most one can say that these studies show some similarity in the factors derived from Varimax rotations when similar items (types of activities) are included in different studies, though formal factor structure comparisons show major differences as well (Schmitz-Scherzer et al., 1974). We suggest that greater similarity would emerge if principal components results were reported regularly and if similar broad ranges of leisure and recreational activity measures were used.

As Beaman (1975) notes, factor analysis is not always justified in the attempt to find covariation among leisure and recreational activities. Factor analysis assumes that there are underlying dimensions of activity that all people have in common in one's sample. If this assumption is not met, or if one doubts its validity, one should instead (or also) use cluster analysis in searching for covariation. Several studies have done this, including earlier ones by Beaman himself. Thus Ditton, Goodale, and Johnsen (1975) do a cluster analysis of water-related recreational activities for a sample of northeast Wisconsin household heads, finding clusters of nonparticipants and average participants as well as some activity specialists (people who participate highly in only one activity) and several activity generalist types (people who participate highly in various specific sets of multiple activities). Tatham and Dornoff (1971) and Romsa (1973) do similar cluster analyses of outdoor recreation activities with similar results: People tend to participate not at all or else in clusters of activities, with few highly active "specialists" in a particular type of recreational activity. Romsa finds that only swimming has a significant single activity cluster of persons (that is, of swimming "specialists").

Using national sample Canadian data, Romsa and Girling (1976) focus only on participants in various outdoor recreation activities, disaggregating people into deciles for each activity. When this is done, they find that for all 18 activities, 40% or more of annual activity trips are accounted for by the top decile and over 60% by the top two deciles. Relative to the total sample of participants and nonparticipants in various activities, a small minority account for all of the outdoor recreation activity in most activity types (with the exception of picnics and cookouts, driving for pleasure, and walking and hiking). Sociodemographic characteristics do not effectively distinguish the most active decile of persons in an activity from less active participants, nor do they effectively differentiate among persons in the top decile on different activities. The authors interpret this set of results as indicating the presence of distinct frequency types for recreational activities. In our view these results also indicate the possibility of covariation among activities in degree of participation, though the direct statistical analysis on this point is lacking (that is, an analysis of the degree of overlap among persons in the top deciles on each activity).

A few studies relate sport or outdoor recreational activity to only one or two other kinds of activity, finding the expected covariation (Engstrom, 1974, for physical recreation activity during leisure time and school sport or studies success; Orthner, 1976, for joint leisure activities and marital task sharing during the 6th-11th years of marriage; Stensaasen, 1974, for participation in a special sport program and participation in competitive school sport or school clubs). More convincing are the studies that relate sport or outdoor recreational activity to various other kinds of discretionary social participation, finding covariation among them as predicted by the General Activity Pattern. These results appear in small and specialized sample studies relating high leisure activity levels to work involvement and family involvement (Willmott, 1971), to work involvement, political involvement, and voluntary group participation (Torbert & Rogers, 1973), and to performance levels in various life roles including work, parent, spouse, homemaker, friend, citizen, and voluntary group member (Havighurst

& Feigenbaum, 1959). But larger and more representative samples with a wide variety of measures of discretionary time activities show similar results, both in the U.S. and in other nations using national samples in several cases (Anderson et al., 1969; Curtis & Milton, 1973; Hobart, 1975; Kuhl et al., 1966; McKechnie, 1974; ORRRC, 1962b; Wippler, 1968). Though there is some variation among studies in results, in general these studies indicate that sport and outdoor recreational activities are positively associated with other discretionary social participation such as crafts and hobby activities, political activity, religious participation, formal voluntary group activity, interpersonal activity with friends, reading books/magazines/newspapers, attending movies/museums/lectures/plays/concerts, attending sport events, visiting with relatives, and so on. The major exceptions among frequent discretionary activities are watching TV and listening to the radio (Curtis & Milton, 1973; Kuhl et al., 1966; ORRRC, 1962b).

It is very striking that most of the foregoing studies seem not to notice or grasp the importance of such covariation nor its implications for a General Activity Pattern. One exception is the Curtis and Milton (1973) study, a secondary analysis of national sample Canadian data on youth and adults aged 14 years and over. These authors perceive, where others have not, the general importance of covariation among discretionary time activities. They use the concept of "centrality" to make sense of this situation, defining the term as an individual's degree of integration into the community and the number of ties the person has to the wider community. The availability of resources of all kinds is seen to make for higher centrality, although there are probable ceiling effects hypothesized as well as the possibility of activity specialists. What is most important, perhaps, is that the authors show sport and physical recreational activity to be positively associated with community event attendance and other activities even with statistical controls for education, sex, age, and marital status. The general results here are seen by the authors not only as a result of differential opportunities but also differential socialization and differences in personality and psychological factors (attitudes, etc.) that make for differential selection effects. This analytical approach is very close to the more fully explicated General Activity Pattern presented by the first author in the first part of Smith and Macaulay (1980), following up on earlier work (Smith, 1969).

Finally, there is even some longitudinal evidence for a General Activity Pattern in the recreation and sport literature, though much more is needed. LaPage and Ragain (1974) report an 8-year panel survey of camping families, finding that as years of inactivity increase since last camping, people are less likely to return to this activity. A declining trend in camping activity is associated with an initial low level and with an exploratory style of camping (rather than return visits to the same sites), though also with resource factors. In a cross-sectional study of male retirees in four Arizona retirement communities, Bultena and Wood (1970) also find that postretirement leisure activity levels are associated with preretirement formal voluntary group activity levels while residing elsewhere in the U.S. The more convincing evidence on this point, however, comes from a longitudinal study of adults aged 40-70 years (Havighurst, 1961), which shows that higher status people retain more interest and vigor in leisure activities of various kinds as they get older, while lower status people are more likely to reduce both their interests and activities. These results are consistent with the Bultena and Wood study because the respondents of the latter were generally much higher in status than the average U.S. population.

Though these studies are few in number and limited in sampling (and activity focus, for the first one), they support the notion of continuity in general discretionary activity levels for individuals over time but decreasing with advancing age for lower socioeconomic status people. All of this and the prior research cited suggests the presence of a General Activity Pattern that includes sport and outdoor recreational activities as an important component part of the pattern. There are, of course, also very marked differences in discretionary social participation not excepting sport and outdoor recreation. But such differences, reflected in factor and cluster analyses already indicated above, coexist with a more general covariation that cannot be explained away and that is present generally when proper analytical and statistical tools are used to test its existence (for instance, principal components factor analysis prior to rotation of axes). This duality is discussed further in the concluding chapter of Smith and Macaulay (1980).

Although social background and social role characteristics are obviously important factors in understanding sport and outdoor recreational (indeed, all kinds of leisure) activities, there has been a general tendency in the present area of research to overemphasize these kinds of variables to the exclusion of other types of variables. More than 20 years ago, Berger (1963) noted that leisure research has remained ''little else than a reporting of survey data on what selected samples of individuals do with the time in which they are not working and the correlation of these data with conventional demographic variables'' (p. 28). Things have improved somewhat in the interim, but the statement still applies to a substantial degree. In the subsequent chapters of this book we shall review some of the research that has progressed beyond the state of leisure research early in the 1960s. As will be noted from the dates of the studies involved, much of the progress made in looking at more psychological variables came in the 1970s.

# CHAPTER SIX

# *Intellectual Capacities and Personality Traits*

After a brief look at the studies done on the relationship of intelligence to sport and outdoor recreational participation, we will discuss the literature on personality traits. The relation of the General Activity Pattern to further study in this area will be highlighted.

## *Intellectual Capacities*

Although there has been a good deal of research on personality traits in relation to sport and outdoor recreational participation in the past decade or so, the record of research regarding the effects of intellectual capacities on such activities is abysmal. For the very small number of studies that do exist the results are mixed. Higher measured intelligence has been associated with participation in interscholastic sport in the United States (Lueptow & Kayser, 1973; Otto & Alwin, 1977; Rehberg & Cohen, 1976), although generally the magnitude of the association is not great ($r$ = .21 or less). In a related study among Israeli schoolchildren, students chosen on the basis of athletic skills to participate in a sport class had a "significantly higher level" of intelligence than candidates for the class who were not selected; correlation coefficients were not reported (Levin, 1980). Similarly, top athletes in different sports have been found to be above average in intelligence, especially for tests with strong verbal components but also for tests of spatial, reasoning, and visual-perceptual capacities (Stockfelt, 1970). Ogilvie (1974) found top national and world-class athletes to be higher in abstract reasoning ability, a result that Husman (1969) reports is fairly common in his literature review. But other studies, particularly with samples of high school or college athletes compared with nonathletes, find lower intelligence among athletes than among others (Edwards, 1973; Ferris, 1970; King & Chi, 1974; Slusher, 1964), though not by marked degrees. Unfortunately, neither the former nor the latter set of studies has adequately controlled for other possibly confounding variables in arriving at their conclusions, so little confidence can be placed in the results. On the whole, the data suggest lower verbal intelligence among high school or college athletes in intramural sport than among their peers but higher verbal and reasoning abilities among top athletes out of school, whether amateur or professional. Unfortunately these results and the studies they are based on leave much to be desired as far as generalization because they tell us nothing about the relationships of intellectual capacities to sport and outdoor recreational activities among the bulk of the population. There is much need for the latter sort of study.

## Personality Traits

The situation is better regarding the study of personality traits and sport participation, though little better for the study of personality in relation to other kinds of outdoor recreation. The great bulk of the studies focus on either school athletes, the favorite sample type, or on outstanding athletes in a given sport or sports. Very few deal with sport, let alone other outdoor recreation, among the general public in relation to personality. When a sample of the general public is used, the personality trait measures are generally very limited (most focus on some measure of ego strength or adjustment). We have been able to find only three examples of studies using both a fairly broad sample from the general population and a variety of personality trait measures. Even these three are not based on a representative sample of the general population but rather on haphazard samples of participants and nonparticipants in various sport and recreational activities (Hall, 1973; Ibrahim, 1970; O'Connor, 1970). In spite of these major defects, these studies most closely approximate the kind of study that is needed for the present purposes, so it is important to examine their results first.

Hall (1973), with a haphazard sample of mostly English and some Canadian women, finds greater athletic activity to be associated with personality traits of tough-mindedness, self-sufficiency, self-assertiveness, and emotional stability. O'Connor (1970), with a sample of participants in different types of sport or recreational voluntary groups (hiking, Great Books, acting, river touring, women golfers, Toastmistresses [public speaking], barbershop quartets [singing], hospital volunteers, etc.), found most kinds of participants (at least seven of nine groups) to be above national norms on such traits as needs for achievement, autonomy, dominance, exhibition (prestige, recognition), and heterosexuality (and to a lesser extent higher on intraception or self-insight and need for change or new experiences and affiliation need), while lower than the national norms on need for abasement (and to a lesser extent, lower on endurance). These results were pretty consistent, with exceptions occurring mainly for the barbershop quartet singers and hospital volunteers; hence the three outdoor recreation group participants reflect the results noted. Unfortunately, we cannot separate the latter effects, indeed the effects of personality traits for any of the participant groups, from personality effects on voluntary group participation in general.

The third study, by Ibrahim (1970), is similar in using a haphazard sample of participants in various kinds of recreational activities who stated that they only participate in a single activity such as art, athletics, playing bridge, dramatics, fishing, surfing, or a sewing club or sorority. However, unlike the prior study, only those involved in dramatics, the sewing group, or the sorority were formal voluntary group participants in their recreational activity. Rather than testing differences from the national norms, Ibrahim performs one-way analyses of variance among the various types of participants on 10 personality traits, finding significant differences in emotional stability, objectivity (vs. hypersensitivity or self-centeredness), and thoughtfulness (vs. interest in overt activity or mental disconcertedness) for both men and women, and significant differences in sociability (extroversion and need for prestige or recognition) and personal relations (tolerance of other people and faith in social institutions) for men but not women, whereas women showed significant differences for friendliness (toleration of hostile action and respect for others). Small sample sizes for each type make the results unreliable (about 20 persons per type), and the more general question of ours regarding differences between participants and nonparticipants in sport and outdoor recreation is not answered because there is no nonparticipant group for comparison (nor are national norm figures reported).

We report some of the details on the foregoing studies here not because the research involved is exemplary; clearly it is far from it. Rather, we wish to indicate the magnitude of the problem in this type of research. Even when broader population samples and a variety of personality traits have been involved, the haphazard sampling, small sample size, failure to differentiate voluntary group-based from informal recreation, and inadequate statistical analysis combine to make the results of little reliability. If the "best" studies have these problems, it can be imagined how much less reliable are the other studies as a basis for generalization to the total population. Nonetheless, we have reviewed numerous studies relating personality traits to athletic (and sometimes broader recreational) participation, most of them having high school or college student samples, as noted earlier.

Collectively, these studies lead, albeit shakily, to the following conclusions. Sport participation tends to be higher for persons with

- greater extroversion, especially in team rather than individual sport (Chipman, 1968; Davey, 1975; Edwards, 1973; Hendry, 1970; Hendry & Douglass, 1975; Husman, 1969; Kane, 1970; King & Chi, 1974; Kirkcaldy, 1982; Moore, 1969; Niblock, 1967; O'Connor, 1970; Stebbins, 1969; Warburton & Kane, 1966; this conclusion is also reported by Eysenck, Nias, & Cox [1982] in their review of the literature); trait names used here include sociability, group dependence, need for affiliation, communality, trust, outgoingness, coachability, and conformity. Ogilvie (1974) found opposite results in his study of national and world-class top athletes; Fuchs and Zaichkowsky (1983) found that male and female bodybuilders demonstrate a profile no different from that of the general population on this measure.
- greater ego strength and adjustment (Albinson, 1971; Davey, 1975; Edwards, 1973; Hall, 1973; Hendry & Douglass, 1975; Husman, 1969; Kane, 1970; Kelly, 1969; King & Chi, 1974; Moore, 1969; O'Connor, 1970; Ogilvie, 1974; Sessoms & Oakley, 1969; Snyder & Kivlin, 1975; this finding also is reported by Eysenck et al. [1982] in their review); studies with general population samples are supportive here, even with other factors controlled in a few studies, though the dependent variable is at times broader leisure activity rather than narrower sport and outdoor recreational participation (Bley, Goodman, Dye, & Harel, 1972; Bultena & Wood, 1970; Havighurst, 1961; Havighurst & Feigenbaum, 1959; Hobart, 1975; Robinson, 1977; Wippler, 1968); exceptions are rare, but a few reversals are found (Ibrahim & Morrison,

1976; Davey, 1975, for neuroticism only; Slusher, 1964, for hypochondria); trait names used include personal adjustment, lack of neuroticism, self-sufficiency, tough-mindedness, lack of anomie, life satisfaction, self-concept, intraception, self-assurance, socialization, self-acceptance, psychological well-being, body image, lack of anxiety, morale, mental toughness, and confidence.

- greater emotional stability (Davey, 1975; Edwards, 1973; Hall, 1973; Hendry, 1970; Husman, 1969; Kelly, 1969; Niblock, 1967; Ogilvie, 1974; Warburton & Kane, 1966); trait names used include emotional control and poise.
- greater emotional detachment and less emotional closeness (Ogilvie, 1974).
- greater assertiveness (Aamodt, Alexander, & Kimbrough, 1982; Allen, 1982; Chipman, 1968; Davey, 1975; Fletcher, 1970; Fletcher & Dowell, 1971; Hall, 1973; Husman, 1969; Kane, 1970; Kelly, 1969; Niblock, 1967; O'Connor, 1970; Ogilvie, 1974; Winter, 1973); exceptions in the form of reversals are rare (Edwards, 1973, for abasement and deference; Husman, 1969, for aggressiveness); trait names used include dominance, power need, aggressiveness, ascendancy, autonomy need, leadership, independence, and lack of abasement or deference needs.
- greater sense of efficacy and need for achievement (see Davey, 1975; Henschen, Edwards, & Mathinos, 1982; Husman, 1969; Lynn, Phelan, & Kiker, 1969; Moore, 1969; Rehberg & Cohen, 1976); exceptions occur mainly in finding nonsignificance, not reversals (Di Giuseppe, 1973; Gilliland, 1974; Gorsuch, 1968; Hutchinson, 1972), but occasional reversals occur (Fletcher, 1970); trait names used include internal (vs. external) control, achievement via conformance, desire, determination, and environmental mastery.
- greater need for prominence or prestige (Carls, 1969; O'Connor, 1970; Ogilvie, 1974); trait names used include need for exhibition and need for success and recognition.
- greater morality and altruism (Davey, 1975; Moore, 1969); one exception is a reversal when nurturance need (giving help and support) is measured (Ogilvie, 1974), but there are others too (Edwards, 1973); main trait name used is responsibility.
- greater flexibility (Fletcher & Dowell, 1971; O'Connor, 1970); exceptions occur (Edwards, 1973); trait names include need for change and lack of orderliness.
- greater energy level (Niblock, 1967); trait name used is general activity.
- greater deliberateness (Davey, 1975; Edwards, 1973; Fletcher,

1970; Husman, 1969; King & Chi, 1974; O'Connor, 1970; Rehberg & Cohen, 1976); reversals are rare (Fletcher, 1970); trait names used include endurance, conscientiousness, soberness, persistence, lack of impulsivity, future orientation, and conservativeness.

- greater stimulation need (Gould & Landers, 1972; Harris, 1973; Husman, 1969; Loy & Donnelly, 1976; McKechnie, 1974; Ogilvie, 1974; Robinson, 1977); trait names used include need for stress, need for new experiences, need for kinesthetic pleasure, interest in new people, boldness, venturesomeness, and lack of fear of danger.
- greater self-actualization and creativity (Harris, 1973; Ogilvie, 1974); exceptions occur as findings of nonsignificance, not reversals (Ibrahim & Morrison, 1976).

All of the foregoing conclusions are based on rather weak research support, with their relative strength indicated by the number of supporting studies and lack of many exceptions. Some personality traits in the analytical scheme set forth in chapter two of Smith and Macaulay (1980) have apparently not been examined in relation to sport and outdoor recreational participation—curiosity, ego defense mechanisms, and ego expression styles in particular (though the mental toughness and objectivity traits used in some studies might be seen as ego defense mechanisms). Others in that scheme have received so little research attention that the foregoing conclusions must be taken with great caution (notably, for emotional detachment, need for prominence, morality, flexibility, energy level, stimulation need, and self-actualization need). Some studies have included traits that do not fall readily into any category of the scheme. These studies indicate that there is greater sport participation for

- greater masculinity (Kelly, 1969; Slusher, 1964).
- greater heterosexuality (Fletcher, 1970; O'Connor, 1970).
- greater practicality and reality sense (King & Chi, 1974; Ogilvie, 1974); however, this trait might be classified with deliberateness.

The overriding meaning of all of these results regarding sport or recreational participation and personality can be fairly readily summed up by saying that more active participants tend to be characterized by more socially desirable personality traits (see Ferris, 1970, for this suggestion). The only exception (and this based on a single study) is the emotional detachment trait, with some question about whether the stimulation need trait is neutral, desirable, or undesirable. It would be useful to have some research that bears directly on this question of the social desirability of the ends of the various trait dimensions for U.S. and other societies. There are, of course, several studies in which personality traits do not distinguish between athletic participants and nonparticipants (see Berger & Littlefield, 1969; Ferris, 1970), but such studies are usually with samples too small to show anything but very large differences, samples with restricted social background characteristics so that attenuation of effects for the larger population is likely, use of significance tests that are insufficiently powerful (sometimes through setting too low a significance level cutoff or failure to use one-tailed tests for lack of a guiding hypothesis), or focus on a single sport rather than sport and outdoor recreation in general. The foregoing statement holds for most of the studies noted before as "exceptions" indicating nonsignificance of certain traits in relation to sport participation. Given this fact, and the relatively small number of significant reversals noted earlier, one is inclined to conclude that the existing research on personality traits, however inadequate, generally confirms rather strongly that people more active in sport and outdoor recreation (especially high school and college students) tend to have scores significantly more in the socially desirable direction on a variety of personality traits. This is consistent with the predictions of the General Activity Pattern discussed in Smith and Macaulay (1980).

There is a great deal that needs to be done before one can have any real confidence in the empirical relationships between personality traits and sport and outdoor recreational participation, however. What is needed is research on all levels of participation for both sport and outdoor recreational activities of individuals (not just for sport, as is usual so far) for large and representative samples of both youth and adults (not just for large samples, as is usual so far) using a broad variety of personality trait measures rather than only one or two (one or two being usual so far). Measures of social background, contextual, attitudinal, informational, and situational variables should also be included so that they can be examined in multivariate analyses and controlled statistically while attempting to understand the effects (and causes) of personality traits. Existing studies almost never include any of the kinds of statistical controls just noted, the few exceptions being Havighurst and Feigenbaum (1959), who controlled for socioeconomic status in studying the personal adjustment trait; Hobart (1975), who controlled for age and sex in studying anomie (adjustment lack); Bultena and Wood (1970), who controlled for age, health, and social class in studying the life satisfaction (adjustment) trait; and Hall (1973), who performed a multiple regression analysis with several traits and social background variables. It is noteworthy that all of the foregoing studies with statistical controls for other possibly confounding variables gave results supporting the General Activity Pattern predictions and the importance of personality traits for understanding sport and recreational participation. The failure of the large, indeed overwhelming, majority of studies to include these kinds of statistical controls and to perform adequate multivariate analyses is, in our view, another indication of the tendency for social participation research to be discipline, and even subdiscipline, bound, to the detriment of our understanding of the phenomena we are attempting to study. Whether or not one accepts the General Activity Pattern as a reasonable model, the Interdisciplinary Sequential Specificity Time Allocation Lifespan Model (ISSTAL Model) discussed in chapter one and in Smith and Macaulay (1980) is a necessary corrective to the kind of atheoretical and discipline-bound research that predominates in the study of personality in relation to sport and recreational participation. Needless to say, the longitudinal dimension must also be added to the description of needed research given above. The question of selection versus social learning effects has not been properly addressed by empirical research in the present area, a conclusion that is sadly still as true today as it was nearly two decades ago when Husman (1969) reached it after reviewing the literature then extant on sport and personality dynamics. Some few studies, like that of Kane (1970), suggest selection effects are crucial, however.

There are quite a few pieces of research that relate personality traits to participation in specific sports or that attempt to differentiate the personalities of participants in team versus individual sports (Ferris, 1970; Husman, 1969). However, we have not attempted to review such studies here because, like the earlier literature reviewers just cited, we do not feel existing studies add up to anything. Thus, where Husman and Ferris reviewed pre-1970 literature, we have not done so for later literature. The research performed is so inadequate methodologically in ways already noted for more general participant versus non-participant research that no useful purpose would be served here by reviewing it. Doubtless there are some important variations in personality traits associated with the choice of one sport or outdoor recreational activity rather than another. But until and unless a solid empirical research base is built regarding the personality traits of participants in general, we do not believe much progress can be made regarding the traits that distinguish particular types of sport or recreational participants. This is inevitable, in our view, because one must control for the generally active personality profile in attempting to understand what personality traits are associated with a particular activity. That is, specific sport or recreational personality types can only be studied properly as variations from or of the generally active sport and recreational personality type, the latter being defined in terms of the socially desirable end of the various personality trait dimensions in the analytical scheme presented in chapter one of this volume. If one tries to study the personality traits and the levels of them associated with a particular sport without taking account of the more general personality pattern of participants versus nonparticipants for all (or most) kinds of sport and outdoor recreation, one will necessarily confuse elements of the general personality pattern with possible elements of the more specific variation of or from it. For example, if one studies the personality traits of swimmers and finds them to be well adjusted, assertive, and so on, one may actually be studying the personality traits of participants in sport more generally without knowing it (assuming that no other sport participants are included in one's study). Or if one is comparing swimmers with baseball players and runners, the differences in their personalities can only be properly understood against the background of how the personalities of all three (sometimes overlapping) types of participants differ more generally from nonparticipants in sport.

Finally, there are doubtless differences in personality trait measurements associated with participation versus nonparticipation that may vary from differences between highly active or successful participants and less active or successful participants. Existing research on sport and outdoor recreation in relation to personality traits does not examine this issue. We could find no study in which any attempt was made to seek such variations. Instead, studies focus either on the participant versus nonparticipant distinction or on the successful-active participant versus less successful-active participant, but rarely on both. In the few studies where both are examined, other methodological problems make the results dubious and a special review of these studies here superfluous. It has been shown elsewhere (Smith, 1966) that the two levels of participation can have quite different distinguishing variables, including personality traits, when formal voluntary group participation is the focus of inquiry. Similar findings in the area of sport and outdoor recreation are not hard to imagine, any more than variations in the personality traits affecting participation in different sports or outdoor recreational activities are difficult to imagine. Hence, future research must include measures of different levels of participation and analyze such data so that possible variations of the sort just suggested will have an opportunity to show up if they exist. The personality and social structure congruence model will be useful here in suggesting both how different sports may attract (or mold) different specific personality types as well as in suggesting how participation in a sport at all may be determined by traits other than active-successful participation in a given sport or outdoor recreational activity. This model would suggest, for instance, that participants in individual sports are lower on extroversion than participants in team sports because the latter kinds of sports are socially structured to require more interpersonal relations and interdependence. Some research studies cited above under the trait extroversion support this hypothesis. Similarly, the model would suggest that extroversion will be more important as a trait that differentiates participants from nonparticipants in most sport and outdoor recreation than as a trait that differentiates successful-active from less successful-less active participants, because in most types of activities other traits such as the needs for stimulation, prominence, or achievement are likely to determine high success-activity once a person becomes a participant.

# CHAPTER SEVEN

## *Attitudinal Dispositions*

Just as the realm of personality traits has only recently begun to be studied fairly frequently, so too have attitudinal dispositions only lately begun to be studied reasonably frequently in the realm of sport and outdoor recreation. However, attitudinal dispositions have gotten a later start here. For one thing, while personality trait measures can be borrowed from personality psychology research in general, attitudinal disposition measures have had to be created specifically for the realm of sport and outdoor recreation. This process takes a good deal of time to do well, and until it is done well, substantive research on the effects (or causes) of attitudinal dispositions cannot be expected.

# Values

In the sense used here, there has been very little empirical research on how broad individual values relate to sport or outdoor recreational activities. The studies that have been done fall into two main categories: ones that use broad measures of individual values and relate these to participation and ones that ask people about the values or types of satisfactions that leisure or specific sport or recreational activities provide. The first kind of study is more properly reviewed in this section of the present chapter, while the second fits as well into the later section on general and specific attitudes because such studies focus on how the individual perceives and feels about leisure, sport, or outdoor recreation or about a particular activity in these categories. Nevertheless, we shall review some of the latter kind of studies here because they can also be seen as ways of applying broader individual values to particular sports or recreational activities.

A prototypical study of the first kind is that by Lowrey (1969), who applies the Spranger "Types of Men" value test (somewhat modified) to a random sample of adults from an Illinois county. He finds that although there are effects of social background variables, individual values (theoretical, economic, aesthetic, social, political, and religious) have no significant effects on participation in various leisure and recreational formal voluntary groups. This would have been a better, if still possibly fruitless, prototype if informal sport or recreational activities were the dependent variable(s). Some other studies relate one or a few individual value orientations to some kind of recreational participation. Albinson (1971) shows that, among students at a Midwestern university in the U.S., persons higher in physical activity levels had more conservative religious, political, and social values, a more social orientation toward life, and less intellectual-aesthetic orientation to life. Rehberg and Cohen (1976) show that high school students who place a higher value on education are more likely to be active in extracurricular activities, including sport. And Snyder (1969) shows that high school extracurricular activities participation, including sport, is significantly associated with males holding "star athlete" as a valued role model and by females holding "leader in activities" as a valued role model, whereas those holding "brilliant student" as a valued role model were significantly less active (all of this with socioeconomic status and intelligence controlled).

The second kind of study may be exemplified by Donald and Havighurst's (1959) study of adults aged 40-70 years from Kansas City and from New Zealand who were asked what they valued about their leisure activities. In general, the main values that were seen as deriving from leisure activities were intrinsic pleasure of the activity or the activity being a change from one's work. Other values that leisure activities had for people were, in declining order of importance, contact with friends, new experiences, achievement, creativity, and making the time pass. This would be a better example if sport or outdoor recreational activities were more narrowly the focus of inquiry, rather than all leisure activities. However, it is typical in being a study that essentially asks people to describe what satisfactions they derive from participation or what reasons they can give for participating. While at times called values, such satisfactions or reasons are more likely to be called "motivations." In any event, a later report by Havighurst (1961) based on the same data (but using only U.S. data) relates individual differences in values derived from leisure to the amount of leisure activity. He finds that there is more active recreation where people have values of creativity, talent, vitality, and expansion of interests that they derive from their leisure. By performing this additional analysis Havighurst makes the research more than a purely descriptive one. Engstrom (1974), for instance, gathers self-reports of motives for leisure time physical activity from Swedish high school youths, reporting that the principal values mentioned are body condition and health, followed by making the time pass ("alternative to sitting still"), meeting friends, intrinsic pleasure ("enjoyment"), competence, and competition. Anderson et al. (1969) report similar descriptive results from a national survey of Danish youth and adults. They find that active athletes (vs. the more passive people in the sample) are most likely to mention health or comradeship as values when asked why they participate, followed distantly by the values of intrinsic pleasure ("recreation") and competition.

Steele and Zurcher (1973) review the literature on satisfactions from and motivations for leisure, finding 10 major functions or values in the present terms: (a) preparation for life; (b) catharsis; (c) relaxation and recreation; (d) identity generation, reinforcement, and expression; (e) affiliation; (f) separation (from domestic roles or people involved in the latter); (g) socialization; (h) fulfillment of the wishes of others; (i) status and prestige; and (j) occupation (gaining a livelihood). As predicted by the authors, bowlers in a haphazard sample from Austin, Texas, and in the Los Angeles, California area give primarily values that involve b-f (identity generation and affiliation are by far the most frequently given values). The authors argue that because leisure sport and recreational activities are "ephemeral roles," such values as b-f are more likely to be given for any kind of sport or recreational activity. It is this kind of generalization that, although not yet adequately confirmed by a variety of studies, ties the present kind of study to the larger study of values in relation to sport and recreational activities of individuals.

Much more research is clearly needed to explore how values relate to sport and outdoor recreational participation, going beyond merely descriptive studies to analyze how individual values differentially affect participation, with other variables controlled statistically. It is an open question whether and how general individual values apply to sport and outdoor recreation in general or to specific activities. All that is certain is that some few studies have indicated the relevance of differential individual values to participation.

## General Attitudes

The category of general attitudes relevant to sport and outdoor recreational participation is potentially very important, as is the subsequent category of more specific attitudes. Neither category has been much studied, although, like personality traits and like the other types of attitudinal dispositions, they have begun to get increasing attention in the research literature in the past several years. Burdge and Field (1972) made a plea for more research on attitudes and motivation early in the past decade, and this plea may have helped. There is, however, a great deal of confusion evident conceptually regarding whether one is dealing here with values, needs, motivations, perceptions, attitudes, or something else. An example of the conceptual confusion, in our view, would be Mercer's (1973) discussion of "recreational need," in which it is concluded that only felt needs (motivational dispositions in our terminology) as expressed in actual behavior, that is, behavioral regularities, are sufficiently measurable to be useful for research purposes. We could not disagree more strongly, and the research reviewed in the personality traits and attitudinal dispositions chapters of this volume demonstrates that internal psychological dispositions of individuals ("felt needs") are indeed measurable and do seem to affect sport and outdoor recreational participation, as they do any other kind of participation. Rather than ignoring "felt needs" we should instead be trying to better understand and measure them and their effects in the present realm of participation. Heberlein (1973), for instance, suggests that in the study of attitudes one attempt to measure three aspects of each: centrality to one's self and view of reality, vertical structure (logical deductive relationships among attitudes at higher or lower levels of generality), and horizontal structure (linkages among attitudes at the same level of generality). In our scheme presented here, general attitudes and specific attitudes are distinguished by the second aspect—level of generality in terms of logical structures. Heberlein further points out that attitudes are far from perfectly correlated with the corresponding behavior. How much of a correlation there is for sport and outdoor recreational participation forms the central concern of this and the following sections.

One of the main lines of research on leisure and recreational attitudes has been the development of appropriate measuring instruments, as mentioned earlier (e.g., Beard & Ragheb, 1983; Ragheb & Beard, 1982). Neulinger has been one of the leaders in this effort, beginning with a factor analysis of 68 attitude items regarding leisure performed on a haphazard sample of New York City area residents. The result of that study (Neulinger & Breit, 1969) was a set of seven factor-derived scales labeled as follows: amount of work or vacation desired, society's role in leisure planning, self-definition through work or leisure, amount of perceived leisure, autonomous versus passive leisure activities, affinity to leisure (liking for a life of leisure), and importance of public approval (which is really need for prominence, a personality trait, in our opinion). In a subsequent study on a similar kind of haphazard sample, Neulinger and Breit (1971) report a partial replication of their earlier study, based on a factor analysis of 27 items from that study plus 5 new items designed to "get at the essence" of the earlier factors. In this study, five factors are derived that are similar to ones from the earlier study, namely all but autonomous versus passive leisure activities and the importance of public approval (which never belonged in an attitude scale in the first place). In his book Neulinger (1974) reports these results again and makes a well-taken plea for a national sample attitude survey, though hopefully it will include some other variables discussed in this chapter as well and will make an attempt to relate various general leisure attitudes to leisure behavior of various kinds, sport and outdoor recreation included. A more recent study with a sample of students further replicates the factor structure of the second study above (Neulinger, Light, & Mobley, 1976). The major problem with this series of studies is that only a minority of the attitude variance (merely 38% in the 1971 study, for instance) is accounted for by the five Varimax factors derived. This leaves the majority of leisure attitude variance out of the factors and scales dealt with. It is also unfortunate that, so far, no studies of the explanatory-predictive validity of these attitude clusters or scales have been published, nor have reliability figures been made available. Still, it is a start in the right direction.

Another similar line of research was initiated by Kenyon, who developed a model for physical activity attitudes in six subdomains: physical activity as social experience, health and fitness pursuit, pursuit of vertigo (thrill), aesthetic experience, recreational experience (catharsis and tension release), and ascetic experience (deferred gratification and testing of one's powers). Kenyon (1968) uses data on college students to demonstrate the existence of these various subdomains as separate factors derived from an oblique rotation factor analysis. However, all six attitude factor scales are also intercorrelated positively and usually significantly, making a total scale score for leisure attitudes reasonable to compute. A manual for these scales (adding "game of chance" attitudes) was later published (Kenyon, 1972), and Fisher and Driscoll (1975) have shown that male high school students who are athletes have higher total positive physical activity scale scores than nonathletes, giving some validation to the attitude scales.

Still another similar attempt to derive multiple general attitude scales in this area is the work of McKechnie (1974), who devised six attitude scales measuring pastoralism (appreciation for and preservation of a primitive natural environment), urbanism (appreciation of city life and culture for recreation), environmental adaptation (people manipulating nature), environmental trust (vs. fear of the environment), antiquarianism (preservation of old human artifacts of various kinds), and mechanical orientation (appreciation of mechanical objects and technological processes). When these scales were correlated with various factor-derived scales of leisure and recreational participation, the following results emerged: Pastoralism was significantly positively correlated with five of six types of leisure participation, with only a "slow living" (mass media use, visiting, gardening, etc.) factor scale excepted. Hence, pastoralism was associated with two participation scales that involve extensive sport and outdoor recreational participation (neighborhood sport and glamour sport). Environmental trust showed similar significant positive correlations with the participation scales, especially with the sport and outdoor recreation participation scales. Antiquarianism had low positive correlations with participation scales generally and was statistically significant for females in relationships with the crafts, intellectual (high culture), neighborhood, and glamour sport participation scales. Mechanical orientation was strongly related with a "mechanics" participation scale (metalworking, auto mechanics on own car, fishing, hunting, etc.) for men and with crafts participation for both men and women. Environmental adaptation was little related to anything, except negatively with the "intellectual" participation scale. A representative sample of adults from a California county provided the data involved.

Other researchers have used narrower general attitude scales to study sport and outdoor recreational participation, usually finding at least some significant relationships between attitudes and participation. Examples here would include Snyder and Spreitzer (1974), who found general attitudes toward sport (termed "affective involvement") to be moderately strongly correlated with a broad measure of sport participation that included attending sport events and reading about sport as well as direct involvement. They did not find sport participation to be significantly related to attitudes regarding the meaning of work and leisure, however, in their sample of adults from Toledo, Ohio. Hendry and Douglass (1975) found more favorable attitudes to physical recreation for Scottish university students who were more involved in sport activity, using the Kenyon (1972) scales mentioned earlier. Dowell (1973), Engstrom (1974), and Stensaasen (1974) found similar results for samples of college and grade school youth from the U.S., Sweden, and Norway, respectively, using different measures of positive general attitudes toward physical recreation or sport. Spreitzer and Snyder (1983) found sportspeople to be higher in their perception of their own sports abilities and pride than the general population. Sportspeople were also more likely to see leisure as compensatory for work.

Studies with adult samples of various kinds also indicate that positive general leisure, sport, or recreational attitudes are significantly and positively associated with sport or outdoor recreational participation (Christensen & Yoesting, 1973, 1976; Hall, 1973; Harris, 1970; Wippler, 1968; Yoesting & Burkhead, 1973). Some of the latter are particularly convincing because they show that attitudes toward recreation have significant effects even in multiple regression analyses when social background variables are controlled. For instance, Wippler (1968) found positive attitudes toward the outdoors to be the strongest predictor of an outdoor recreation participation scale with other social background factors controlled and involved in the stepwise regression equation (his sample was a representative one for adults of the province of Groningen, Netherlands). Also of interest is the finding by Robinson (1977), with an urban sample, that higher satisfaction (attitude) with games and sport was significantly correlated with watching sport, playing active sports, hunting and fishing, and even playing cards and other games. Other findings here are those discussed in the earlier section on socialization concerning the relationship between orientations toward games and sport and prior experiences. It will be recalled that play-oriented attitudes toward sport were associated with more informal and unorganized participation, while organized participation more often led to an orientation that stressed winning.

From a different perspective, Knopp and Tyger (1973) show that Minnesota skimobile users and ski-touring participants in the same recreational areas have markedly different general attitudes toward environmental issues, although both groups tend toward the "environmentalist image" in their views. They also have differences in attitudes toward the controlled use of public lands (with ski tourers being more favorable to this). However, there were important social background variable differences between the two groups as well, and these were not controlled in looking at attitudes, a not uncommon failing in the attitude research being reviewed here. Job attitudes have also been examined in relation to sport and outdoor recreational participation, with mixed results. Grubb (1975) found more participation in outdoor recreation perceived to be stimulating where auto assembly line workers had more job boredom attitudes; similarly, Wippler (1968) found a sense of greater pressure at work (hence, presumably more involvement) to be associated significantly with less outdoor recreation (a result holding up with minor significance even in a multiple regression analysis). But Bacon (1975) found no significant relationships in his work attitude study. Finally, it is of interest to note that Anderson (1959), in a longitudinal study of men 20-59 years of age using the Strong Vocational Interest Blank, found that there was a marked decline with age of interest in (favorable general attitudes toward) physical skill, daring, and strenuous physical activity; however, interest in solitary and more sedentary activities increased with age. This study thus gives some psychological underpinning to the frequent result, noted earlier, that sport and outdoor recreational activity tend to decline markedly with age. Clearly the attitudes and the participation decline together, though no study we know of shows the direction of causality involved (again because of insufficient longitudinal study).

To sum up, there is solid evidence that general attitudes toward leisure, sport, and outdoor recreation are associated in the expected direction with corresponding participation, even when other variables such as social background are controlled. There is a great deal more work to be done here before the full implications of general attitudes are understood in relation to sport and outdoor recreational participation, however. It is particularly important to explore the full range of such attitudes as they might affect participation in general and participation in particular activities, with a similarly full range of other types of variables controlled, and all of this done with large and representative samples of the general population. So far, no study we are aware of has even come close to doing this, in the U.S. or elsewhere.

## Specific Attitudes

Specific sport and outdoor recreation attitudes focus on particular sports or recreation activities or small subsets of activities, rather than dealing with leisure, sport, or outdoor recreational attitudes more broadly. Specific attitudes also focus on particular sites of sport or outdoor recreation, not just activities themselves. There is only a very modest amount of research on these kinds of attitudes in the sport and outdoor recreation field, the great majority of it recent. Donald and Havighurst (1959) perhaps began this line of research by showing that very different meanings were given to 11 leisure activities by their sample of adults aged 40-70 years from Kansas City. Goodale (1965) also contributed to this research line by showing a variety of specific attitude factors existed for his sample of adults from 12 Minneapolis census tracts: program satisfaction in the Minneapolis area, satisfaction with park and recreational facilities in one's neighborhood, a neighborhood orientation toward leisure time, and a general attitude toward the importance of parks and recreation (that is, a broader attitude that fit better with the research reviewed in the prior section). In an analysis of variance he found that the people from the 12 census tracts differed significantly both in recreational activity levels as well as in specific park and recreational attitudes.

More recently, Snyder, Spreitzer, and Kivlin (1975) have shown that various sports show distinctive gender role stereotyping attitudes, such that women are not supposed to participate in certain sports (track and field, softball, basketball) while participation in other sports is acceptable for them (swimming, tennis). Such specific sport attitudes are clearly the product of socialization rather than individual preferences, for they are found among both males and females irrespective of one's own participation in a given sport in the sample of Toledo, Ohio adults studied.

As mentioned earlier in this chapter in discussing values and participation, the reasons or motivations reported by individuals for participating or not in a particular sport or recreational activity can be viewed as falling into the present category of specific attitudes, whatever these measures may be called by investigators using them. Tinsley, Barrett, and Kass (1977), for instance, speak of leisure activities being associated with different kinds of "need satisfaction." They measure 45 types of need satisfaction for five leisure activities (attending plays/concerts/lectures, reading books/magazines, watching TV, bicycling, and drinking/socializing) using 302 specially designed items for each activity. Different sets of their college student respondents rated different ones of the five leisure activities in terms of how well they satisfied the various needs, and a mean level of need satisfaction was computed for each of the 45 needs, based on the subset of respondents who had rated a given leisure activity for the various need satisfaction possibilities. When an analysis of variance was then performed on each of the 45 need satisfaction (specific attitude) means for the five activity type groups, 42 of the 45 were statistically significant, and nearly half were deemed a difference large enough to be substantively meaningful. The strongest results were for six need satisfaction types:

There was more sex need satisfaction perceived as probable from drinking and socializing; more catharsis probable from bicycling; more independence from reading and bicycling; more understanding from reading and from attending plays/concerts/lectures; and more getting along with others from drinking and socializing, as well as more probable affiliation need satisfaction. Reliabilities for all but one of the need satisfaction mean scales were satisfactory. This study is striking in showing the degree of specific attitude differentiation that is possible among leisure and recreational activities, if one cares to go to sufficient lengths to examine it. The procedure is very tedious but may well be necessary for every sport and recreational activity if we are ever to understand precisely why people participate or not in such activities and how specific activity attitudes fit into the overall picture of explanation.

An approach that is generally overlooked focuses on the degree of commitment by the participant to a leisure activity. An example of this would be the work of Spreitzer and Snyder (1983) in which they show that participants in a 10-k road race or in a racquetball tournament have greater commitment to adult sports participation than does the general public. The commitment tapped here is clearly an attitude, and a specific one insofar as it pertains to specific leisure activities.

Less refined approaches to understanding specific attitudes of individuals toward particular sport or outdoor recreational activities involve the several studies that examine the reasons people give for participation in particular activities. An early study of this sort was Etzkorn's (1964) study of campers arriving at a campground north of Los Angeles who were asked why they were camping there and what they like about camping. The results, when coded, indicated that rest and relaxation, meeting congenial people, and living the outdoor life were the most common types of responses. This indicates that the campers had specific attitudes toward camping as an activity that inclined them to expect those kinds of satisfactions to ensue from participation. Reviewing the earlier studies using the national U.S. sample data gathered by the ORRRC in the early and mid-1960s, Cicchetti (1972) notes that the main reasons people gave for not participating at all in a desired outdoor recreation activity (had a specific attitude toward such an activity) were that facilities were too crowded, money or equipment was lacking, time was lacking, or they lacked the ability (in their view) to participate.

Although each of these specific attitudes is doubtlessly related fairly well to objective resource or ability factors, the specific attitudes mediate between the objective factors and actual nonparticipation by the individual, and the relationship between objective factors and individual specific attitudes corresponding to such factors is probably far from perfect (though this matter has not been studied, to our knowledge). Cicchetti also notes that the reasons given by people for not participating more in desired activities mainly related to time but also included some of the other "barriers" noted above. Nix (1969) reports results of a much more modest study of students from five California high schools, indicating the various reasons why athletes and nonathletes stated they did or did not get involved in sport. Several other studies have delved more deeply into the reasons people give for camping in particular (Clark, Hendee, & Campbell, 1971; Hollender, 1977; Taylor & Knudson, 1973), but none of these relate specific camping attitudes to the differential camping behavior of campers and noncampers (for lack of a noncamper sample, usually).

The Hollender study is particularly interesting, however, in being a factor analysis of 42 questionnaire items designed to get at different aspects of specific camping attitudes (stated satisfactions or motives). It drew upon earlier descriptive studies such as those noted above and upon subjective interviews with campers. The major factors that emerge are primitive life-style, aesthetic outdoor experiences, escape from urban stress, escape from the familiar (mass media and news of problems), liking to fish, and liking to read books. The factor structure was replicated more or less in two samples, one of college students and one of campers. This study is striking because it shows what can be done in the way of developing specific attitude scales for a given type of sport or outdoor recreation, going beyond the mere descriptive classification of reasons people give for their participation. With such measurement scales, it becomes possible to investigate systematically and rigorously the impact of specific attitudes upon participation or nonparticipation in a particular sport or outdoor recreation, again controlling for other possibly confounding variables. This is the next step to be taken with scales such as Hollender has developed.

And more generally, similar kinds of specific attitude scales need to be developed from informal descriptive material for each and every kind of sport or outdoor recreation activity if we are to be able, ultimately, to understand the reasons why people participate in them and particularly the effects of specific attitudes in determining (or resulting from) such participation. Admittedly this is a very large task, but there is no gainsaying its necessity. The studies that are able to account for even 50% of the variance in any kind of sport or recreational activity for the general population are exceedingly rare, and something must account for the observed participation—possibly little explored variables like specific attitudes. Earlier work with specific attitudes in the study of voluntary group participation demonstrates that such variables can be of substantial importance in multivariate analyses including other types of variables in an analytical scheme.

Another line of research on specific attitudes deals not so much
with attitudes toward specific activities themselves but with attitudes
toward specific sites for those activities. Taylor and Knudson (1973)
report data from interviews with state park campers in eight Midwestern states that indicate why people prefer (that is, have positive
specific attitudes toward) their favorite campsites. Although the results
are merely descriptive, they suggest the possible kinds of scales that
need to be constructed to get at activity site attitudes: closeness to
home, scenery, facilities, and so on. When asked why they did not
visit their favorite sites more often, the campers' outstanding reason
was distance, followed by cost, lack of information, poor facilities,
climate, and poor access. These results are striking in their parallels
to the kinds of site attractiveness measures that researchers concerned
with recreational travel behavior have been devising and using with
substantial success. As noted earlier, distance from one's home to a
recreational travel site is by far the most important determinant of flows
of visitors from a given area to a recreational area more than 30 miles
or so away (O'Rourke, 1974). However, the attractiveness of the site
to be visited is also important, although most recreational travel
researchers have not measured this directly through individual specific
attitudes to sites.

A major exception, then, is the study by Murphy (1975), who
studied recreational boating decisions for residents of Columbus, Ohio.
He carefully controls objective distance (roughly, both sites were nearby), lake size, and site facilities by careful selection of the two sites
to be studied, so that specific attitudinal differences are likely to be
the major factors affecting differential use of the sites. Each site is
then rated by the respondents on five semantic differential-type dimensions: nice-awful, pleasant-unpleasant, good-bad, beautiful-ugly, and
friendly-unfriendly. Number of visits to a given site during a 2-month
period is then shown to be strongly associated with specific attitudes
toward the two sites, controlling for sociodemographic variables, travel
time to site, and the relative attractiveness of the other site to the individual (as measured by relative frequency of visiting the other site
for boating). In a stepwise multiple regression on the full sample of
174 boaters (interviewed as they launched their boats at one or the other
site), seeing the other site as "unfriendly" and the present site as
"nice" accounted for about 21.6% of the variance (the former much
stronger than the latter). When similar analyses were performed on
subsamples disaggregated by three social stratum levels, increasing
amounts of variance were accounted for as the stratum level decreased,
but specific attitudes toward the two sites, less frequency of visits to
the alternative site, and less travel time to the site were uniformly
important predictors for all strata.

Although specific site attitudes can derive from idiosyncratic differences in experiences, such attitude variations can also be affected by objective differences in the nature of the sites involved. Murphy (1975), in the study just cited, controlled such objective site differences, but others have attempted to measure them in precise ways. Carls (1974), for instance, attempts a quantitative measurement of scenic beauty using large photos of Illinois outdoor recreation scenes and having respondents rank them in terms of attractiveness. A multivariate analysis indicates that about 48% of the variance in individual photo preferences can be accounted for by the area of stream, waterfall, or lake in the pictures, together with the smallness of the number of people and lesser degree of human development or artifacts in the photos. The latter two variables, omitted from similar earlier research by others (Shafer, Hamilton, & Schmidt, 1969; Shafer & Tooby, 1972), account for about 20% of the variation in preferences themselves. Lane, Byrd, and Brantley (1975) perform similar research with photos but also include on-site preference ratings. They, too, find sites with water to be preferred, especially when rated in person. But they also find that ratings from photos and in person tend to differ significantly, with photo ratings usually showing higher site preference ratings (perhaps from idealization effects). Thayer, Hodgson, Gustke, Atwood, and Holmes (1976) extend this line of research by showing that ratings (specific attitudes) for scenic beauty are not based on the same criteria for scenic ugliness. Beauty is not the absence of ugliness, nor vice versa. The prior research cited above is actually concerned with scenic beauty, but scenic ugliness has not yet been properly studied, so that the factors determining it are not now clear. (See also Craik, 1973, for additional research on scenic beauty measurement.) Kreimer (1977) offers a critique of the methods used for studying environmental preferences (specific site attitudes), suggesting that photo rating methods have many defects, however practical this general approach may be for the researcher. He suggests that future studies with photos be supplemented with the use of site descriptions and survey research and that the use of photos per se be made more rigorous by the introduction of strict controls for such extraneous variables as weather, season, time of day, composition, view angle, and so on. We would add that there is a great need for merging this kind of site attractiveness research with the recreational travel behavior research tradition, so that we can understand how much specific site attitudes affect actual participation. Further, it will be important to merge the kind of specific attitude research performed by Murphy (1975) on site attractiveness with the scenic beauty (and, eventually, ugliness) research approach. Research is also needed on specific attitudes toward one's home environment as a sport and recreation site.

There are other kinds of site specific attitudes that have received little or no attention from researchers, in spite of successful attempts by some researchers to show their relevance as objective site characteristics in relation to recreational travel. For instance, we are aware of no studies of specific attitudes toward site access, site recreational facilities, or site travel costs (in time, effort, money, etc.) in relation to one's home, on-site recreational costs, nearness of site to alternative or complementary sites, or the variety of recreational activities that can be performed at a given site; yet all of these have been shown to affect recreational travel flows as objective site characteristics (in research to be reviewed under the subsequent chapter heading of "retained information").

There has been a small amount of research on the effects of certain other kinds of specific activity attitudes upon participation. The ORRRC (1962a) had data gathered that showed, for various summer outdoor recreational activities, that specific preferences for particular activities were positively associated with participation in the given activity (and sometimes with other activities as well), using a large national sample from the U.S. The most powerful effect observed was for people with at least some stated preference for an activity to engage in at least one or more days of that activity during the summer period studied. However, degree of preference for an activity was less systematically associated with number of days of participation. A positive association here was observed only for swimming, fishing, camping, and hunting, but not for boating, picnicking, driving, sight-seeing, or bicycling. Hence these results indicate that the impact of specific activity preferences upon participation versus nonparticipation in an activity is more powerful and consistent than their impact upon degree of participation once involved.

This is precisely the kind of effect we were suggesting earlier might also be present for personality trait variables. It might also be present for other psychological and social background variables. Burdge (1969) and Hendricks (1971) are among the few subsequent researchers to indicate similar results for the general relationship between specific activity attitudes and actual participation in a given activity. Unfortunately, in none of these few studies are multivariate analyses performed controlling for the effects of other variables upon participation. Hence, there is a great deal of research that must be done before one can begin to be reasonably certain of the effects of specific attitudes toward sport or outdoor recreational activities and sites upon actual participation.

# *Expectations*

Expectations and expectancies for reinforcement (rewards and satisfaction) from engaging in particular sport or outdoor recreational activities at specific sites with specific other persons have received very little research attention. The same is true for normative expectations held by individuals regarding participation in particular activities and sites with particular persons at particular times. For instance, there seem to be no studies of the impact of normative social expectations upon the present kind of participation with direct measures of both variables. The closest a study comes to this approach is Kaplan's (1960) incidental finding that participation levels in games and sport generally exceed reported enjoyment levels, so that some kind of social pressure effect might be inferred. Kaplan also notes a variety of social role contexts in which various kinds of leisure participation take place.

It is very strange that no one has bothered to examine directly the effects of normative expectations for these contexts upon individual leisure and recreational participation. Perhaps leisure researchers are too concerned with the intrinsic rewards of leisure activities, so that the pressure of normative social expectations is ignored as irrelevant. Such an assumption is based on little supporting data. It flies in the face of a vast body of research showing in general that human beings are eminently social animals responding to learned social norms and normative expectations in virtually every kind of situation seriously studied.

On the issue of expectancies regarding the outcomes of particular sport or recreational behavior, there is at least a small amount of research. The specific and general attitude research cited earlier is to some degree relevant here, though more general in nature. For instance, the research of Tinsley et al. (1977) deals with expectations for need satisfaction whenever a given activity is engaged in as recreation. In the present section we are concerned, instead, with expectations for satisfactions if a given activity is engaged in at some specific time and place under specific circumstances. That is, the present concept of expectations is even more specific to a particular configuration of circumstances than are specific attitudes (hence the term "sequential specificity" in the name for the ISSTAL analytical scheme), let alone general attitudes, values, or personality traits.

An early example of the kind of research needed here is the study by Aronson and Carlsmith (1962), where performance (participation) expectancy is shown to be significantly and positively associated with actual performance. More recently, Senters (1971) studied a small number of shuffleboard players over an 18-month period, focusing on the players' views of the "stakes" (consequences of the activity in terms of satisfactions) and "uncertainty" (probability of particular consequences of the activity). His observations suggest that the players were involved in shuffleboard primarily for intrinsic pleasure until they became relatively skilled. Then they would try to increase the stakes through competition and betting and to increase the uncertainty to a moderate level by not playing very well at first with poorer players, then trying very hard to catch up and win by a small margin.

Csikszentmihalyi (1975a, 1975b) presents a general theory of play that incorporates such findings and other research, including his own, in an attempt to explain why and when play is enjoyable. The key concept in his theory is the "flow experience," in which the individual in a specific recreational activity situation attempts to create an optimal balance of activity opportunities (challenges) and activity capabilities (skills). When the two are in approximate balance, enjoyment is optimized because uncertainty of outcome is optimized; as individuals gain more skill in an activity over time, they tend to raise the level of challenge accordingly. Data on rock climbers, chess players, dancers, basketball players, music composers, and others support this notion. The flow experience is enjoyable because the individual is able to concentrate on a limited stimulus field, forgetting his or her own problems and separate identity, thus transcending ego boundaries and developing a feeling of psychic integration and control over the environment.

Orlick (1974) has also done research on the importance of expectancies in explaining children's play activities. In his study (Orlick, 1973) of Canadian sky divers (parachutists), hockey players, and skiers together with nonparticipants (haphazard sample), he found participation in sport and recreational activities to be a function of positive and negative expectancies regarding the consequences of participation, expectations by others, and expected reactions of others to one's own performance. He views these, in turn, as resulting from prior experiences with a given activity or related activities, positive or negative in terms of satisfactions. He also notes that there are national variations in social norms and expectancies regarding the outcomes of sport and recreational participation, with less competitive emphasis and more emphasis on pleasurable experiences in mainland China than in the U.S. This kind of research on expectancies, combining the social and normative expectations approach with the probability of satisfying outcomes expectancy approach, needs to be performed much more frequently and systematically. However, it must also be done in such a way that it takes account of all of the other possible explanatory variables that we are considering in this volume. Otherwise, what appear to be effects of expectations may in fact be the effects of other confounded variables not measured or controlled statistically in the analysis.

## *Intentions*

As noted in the second chapter of Smith and Macaulay (1980), there is very little research on intentions in relation to social participation generally. Thus it should come as no surprise that there are no studies whatsoever on the effects of intentions on sport or outdoor recreational participation, so far as we are able to tell. This, then, is a totally undeveloped aspect of sport and outdoor recreation participation research at the present and is much deserving of some empirical research attention.

# CHAPTER EIGHT

# Retained Information and Situational Variables

One of the more neglected areas of sport and outdoor recreation research has been the effects of retained information and situational variables on recreational participation. We feel that a great deal of insight could be gained by investigation of these factors.

## Retained Information

As with some other areas of sport and outdoor recreation research, the study of how retained information affects individual participation is in its infancy. The state of knowledge here is so rudimentary that it makes little sense to differentiate among images, beliefs, and knowledge, as suggested by the analytical scheme in Smith and Macaulay (1980). None of the research that has been done makes any such differentiations, nor is it possible to infer from the published reports which of these three categories of information is involved in a particular study. Perhaps the clearest indirect evidence of the importance of retained information as a determinant of individual participation is the body of research dealing with recreational travel. We have cited some of this literature earlier but mention it again here to emphasize its implications for the importance of retained information as a determinant of individual behavior.

In this kind of study (as reviewed, for instance, by O'Rourke, 1974), the dependent variable is the number of visitor trips, aggregated for some county or other territorial unit of origin, to a particular outdoor recreation site (though one could also use the same kind of methods to understand recreational travel to indoor recreational sites). Numerous studies have demonstrated beyond any shadow of doubt that distance from one's place of residence (origin) to a particular recreation site is the most important determinant of how many recreation trips will be made from a particular territorial unit to a particular outdoor recreational site (Beaman, 1974, 1976; Cesario, 1975; Cheung, 1972; Deacon, Pigman, & Deen, 1972; Freund & Wilson, 1974; Johnston & Elsner, 1972; Lentnek, Van Doren, & Trail, 1969; McKillop, 1975; O'Rourke, 1974; Wilkinson, 1973; Wolfe, 1972).

These same studies, and others not cited, show that recreational travel is also affected significantly by the perceived relative scenic beauty (or ugliness) and other aspects of the attractiveness of the recreational site, the travel route, and one's place of residence, together with such matters as travel costs, travel time, on-site costs, and so on. Mercer (1971b) notes there is evidence that distance can sometimes be perceived as a positive factor rather than a negative one (see also Beaman, 1974, 1976; Wilkinson, 1973; Wolfe, 1972). Lentnek et al. (1969) report that activity-specialized boaters tend to choose the nearest lake usable for their activity regardless of environmental aesthetics.

All of this kind of research clearly leads to the conclusion that individual retained information must be a major factor in recreational travel decisions. The paradox is that retained information by individuals regarding possible recreational sites has almost never been measured directly and related to individual recreational activity. What is needed is research that asks individuals about their images, beliefs, and knowledge regarding such matters as outdoor recreational site attractiveness (scenic beauty, facilities, familiarity, nearby alternative access points, costs, size, etc.), travel route attractiveness, travel costs, alternative recreational sites, perceived distance in miles/time/effort, and so on.

In his excellent review of the role of "perception" in recreational travel behavior, Mercer (1971b) notes that such activity is a function of decision making based on preferences (values, general and specific

attitudes, and expectations, in our terminology) and (retained) information. However, as he also points out, there is very little research
extant on these issues, with far more research needed on "1) the awareness and attitudes of recreationists to particular sites or areas at all
scales; 2) the processes by which they acquire this information; by
extension: 3) the attitudes [and information] of the recreationist [regard-
ing] the immediate home environment; and 4) the relationship between these attitudes [and information] and overt leisure behavior"
(pp. 264-265).

Mercer goes on to indicate that decisions prior to recreational travel
are based on the individual's awareness space or subjective mental map
of reality relevant to current motivational dispositions of all kinds. He
cites some of the few pieces of research that show individual retained
information measures to be related to outdoor recreational behavior.
For instance, Barker (1968) found the perceived nature and degree of
water pollution to have a significant effect upon user evaluations and
space preferences for beach goers in the Toronto region of Canada.
Hecock (1966) found similar results in a study of beach quality evaluation on Cape Cod, Massachusetts. Bultena and Taves (1961) have analyzed images of wilderness areas held by individuals, finding important
variations. Mercer (1971a) himself has done research that shows individual "mental maps" (images) to affect recreational travel behavior
in an urban area of Australia. Indeed, he found that distances are perceived as shorter by individuals in the direction away from the city
center and on routes or to sites that are more familiar.

Other studies further support the importance of retained information as a factor affecting outdoor recreational activity and its location.
Lime (1969) reported that 80% of campers in a Minnesota national forest
had decided on a particular site prior to leaving home, and Taylor and
Knudson (1973) showed that 94% of campers in 16 parks in eight U.S.
Midwestern states were now visiting preferred camping areas they had
visited before or had visited in the past 5 years (that is, preferred areas
for camping were areas with which individuals were having or had
had direct acquaintance). In the latter study, about 8% of campers
indicated they had not visited their preferred campsite more often
because of lack of information.

However, the meaning and nature of retained information for
different kinds of individuals in terms of their social background characteristics can vary markedly. Burdge and Field (1972), in an unpublished
survey, show that low-income persons, especially blacks, perceived
wilderness areas as "any location with trees beyond city limits"—a
definition very different than the average middle- or upper-class person
would have. This kind of result implies that there may be important
methodological problems in representative population sample studies

of outdoor recreation, with apparently common words being inter-preted in uncommon ways by the least educated segment of the population. Sonnenfeld (1966), in a related study, suggests that it is important to distinguish natives of an.area from nonnatives in study-ing their recreational behavior. In his view, natives will have less varied and narrower environmental experiences, on the average, so that their standards will be lower in making quality evaluations of possible out-door recreational sites in their vicinity.

Such variations in evaluation criteria as a function of the extensive-ness of retained environmental information could, of course, be directly measured. Ritchie (1975) has made a start in the latter direction by studying the underlying criteria of judgment used by female home-makers from a Canadian city in classifying pairs of recreational activi-ties as similar or different (4 of the 12 activities involved being outdoor sport or recreation). The results showed the criteria used to be mainly the following: active-passive, individual-group involvement, simple-difficult to perform, and involving versus merely time-filling activity. Finally, in a very interesting study, Adams (1971) shows that the deci-sion to travel to a New England coastal beach is related to individual evaluations of the accuracy of weather information, currently predicted and actual on-site weather conditions, and factors affecting beach users' tolerance of suboptimal weather conditions (such as the length of time the trip had been planned in advance or the size of the group of people going).

A few other kinds of studies also make a case for the importance of retained information as a factor affecting individual participation in sport or outdoor recreation. Recall, for instance, that aspects of the self-concept and body image have been found to be related to sport activ-ity by those studying personality traits (Albinson, 1971). And several researchers have argued that the importance of prior, especially child-hood, experiences as determinants of current participation is a result of pleasant current memories of those earlier experiences (Burch, 1969; Burch & Wenger, 1967; Hendee, 1969). From this viewpoint, all of the research reviewed earlier regarding the impact of prior experiences upon sport or outdoor recreational participation may be indirect evi-dence of the importance of retained information. Because the measures of prior experiences are almost invariably retrospective self-reports at the time of the study, the foregoing type of research can actually be considered even direct evidence for the importance of retained infor-mation as a determinant of participation.

Methodologically, more adequate measures of prior experiences would be derived from self-reports or other evidence at the time such experiences occurred, and later related to participation, in a longitudinal study. In this way, prior experiences could be distinguished analytically and methodologically from the effects of retained information (memories) regarding such experiences.

Snyder and Spreitzer (1974) take another approach to retained information that is relevant here. They show that a measure of information ("cognitive involvement"), in this case knowledge of the types of sport celebrity sportspersons are involved in, is strongly associated with individual sport participation (using a broad measure of this variable, including not only active sport involvement but also sport event attendance, talking about sport, reading about sport, etc.).

Finally, Edwards (1973) takes still another approach to retained information. He is concerned with developing a description of the content of American sport ideology (which he terms the "American sports creed"), based on a content analysis of major athletics journals for coaches, as well as newspaper and magazine articles dealing with sport in America. His results indicate that the ideology involves seven central themes and some subthemes: an emphasis on sport as developing character, discipline, competitiveness, physical fitness, mental fitness, religiosity, and patriotism. Reviewing potential evidence for the veracity of this ideology, he concludes that there is little or no evidence to support its truth. Two types of countercreeds that have arisen recently are also discussed: a humanitarian ideology that emphasizes the openness of sport to all and democratic decision-making in sport (in contrast to the current autocratic and hierarchical structures), and an egalitarian ideology that more or less accepts the American creed for sport but requires the elimination of racial and other discrimination in sport (in contrast to widespread current racism and sexism). This approach of Edwards is quite intriguing but needs to be taken further in the future. Measures of individual belief in the various elements of the American sport ideology and its alternatives need to be developed and used as differential predictors of sport and outdoor recreational participation. Hopefully, future research will begin to do this, controlling for other types of possibly confounding variables in the analysis.

## Situational Variables

Variables dealing with the immediate situation and the individual's definition of the situation have been studied very little in relation to sport or outdoor recreational participation. Some of the earlier kinds of variables reviewed in this chapter can be seen as situational variables, especially if one measures them in a very immediate and activity-situation-time-person-specific manner. For instance, the weather variables reviewed earlier could well be placed in the present category. Long-term variations in the weather are indeed contextual variables, but the immediate context of an activity is a situational variable. Similarly, coparticipant status was treated as a social background variable here but could be viewed as an immediate situational variable if the focus was not on habitual patterns and roles but rather upon coparticipants in the immediate situation of an individual's participation. The variables in the expectations and intentions categories (the latter not studied at all yet for sport and outdoor recreation) can also be viewed as virtually situational variables insofar as they are present in the individual's cognition just prior to a particular activity. However, such fineness of differentiation in terms of time and current cognition has not been explored in the present realm of participation.

What has been done that fits directly into the present category of situational variables is very little and far from adequate if we are to understand how such variables affect sport and outdoor recreational participation. Tuan (1974) gives an extensive abstract treatment of environmental perception as affected by symbols and cultural values that change over time, with urbanization and urban-versus-rural differences being major examples of such changes. Craik (1973) reviews a variety of studies on environmental psychology generally, some of which have a bearing on the kinds of situational variables that need to be studied in the present realm. And, as noted earlier, Mercer (1971b) reviews the literature specifically on the role of perception in the recreation experience, with some of the studies involved focusing on situational variables of one or another kind. However, his conclusion is clearly that these kinds of variables have been very inadequately studied in regard to outdoor recreational travel and that much more research is needed.

Such research should attempt to deal with the kinds of stimuli that are immediately present in the individual's conscious awareness or that cause immediate unconscious arousal just prior to sport or recreational decisions (whether to begin, continue, or terminate participation). And this research needs to consider not only external stimuli but also internal somatic as well as psychological stimuli, as suggested in the first chapter of Smith and Macaulay (1980). Finally, such research should try to understand the psychodynamic and cognitive synthesis processes that individuals perform on immediate situational stimuli in order to arrive at current motivational resultants and current definitions of the situation. Lime's (1969) study suggests that such processes may be grouped into four categories for campers traveling to a Minnesota national forest: unconscious, conscious-inexperienced, conscious-experienced, and habitual. It is important to know under what conditions and for what kinds of sport or recreational activities people tend to make these four categories of "decisions." For example, which kinds of sport or outdoor recreational activities do people tend to participate in habitually? In this future research it will be important, as Mercer (1971b) points out, to examine how personal preferences (motivational dispositions of all levels of abstraction, in our terms) affect decision making in the immediate situation. That immediately antecedent situations and experiences are likely to have an effect on sport and outdoor recreational participation when properly studied is suggested in a study by Witt and Bishop (1970). They asked college students if they would feel like participating in 13 different leisure activities (including 3 sport or outdoor recreational activities) immediately after six different types of antecedent situations. Their results showed clear evidence that leisure participation is likely to vary for the same individual according to the nature of the immediately antecedent situation. However, the similarity of the rank orders of activity choices across antecedent situations indicates that more stable activity preferences (such as specific activity attitudes) are probably more important than the antecedent situation, even though the latter has some significant influence.

# CHAPTER NINE

## Conclusions

It is difficult and perhaps pointless to summarize a volume that is itself a summary of the literature. We have tried to give summary statements regarding particular variables and variable types throughout the volume. Therefore, in this final chapter we shall be concerned with how the research literature bears on two theoretical models of the first author, as well as giving a theoretical and methodological critique of the literature we have reviewed on sport and outdoor recreation participation.

In Smith and Macaulay (1980), the first author has presented two models for understanding discretionary time participation by individuals. The first model, the ISSTAL Model, is essentially an accounting scheme for keeping track of all of the many variables that are relevant to explaining participation. Its categories have structured the literature review of this volume. The second model is a more specific variant of the first and is called the General Activity Model. Briefly, this model posits a General Activity Pattern of positive covariation (association) among all kinds of socioculturally valued discretionary behavior, such that one kind of recreational activity, for instance, tends to be associated with participation in other kinds. Further, the General Activity Model posits an underlying set of contextual, social background, and psychological variables that account for the General Activity Pattern, as a result of accommodation of the person to the sociocultural system.

## Support for the ISSTAL Model

From the vantage point of the ISSTAL Model, research on sport and outdoor recreational participation by individuals is still very much in its infancy. Research is very inadequate or even nonexistent in regard to many of the important aspects of the total analytical scheme. However, the research that does exist lends powerful support to the validity of the model or paradigm for understanding, explaining, and predicting sport and outdoor recreational participation. We draw this conclusion because virtually every kind of variable suggested by the ISSTAL Model generally has been found to be significant for an understanding of the present kind of social participation. Intentions are the only kind of variable for which there was absolutely nothing bearing on sport or outdoor recreational participation that we could find, and even here there was a study (Ajzen & Fishbein, 1969) that showed intentions for leisure behavior of other types to be highly predictable from other variables included in the paradigm. If this paradigm were not useful, there would be several types of variables delineated by it that did not seem to have any significant effects upon sport or recreational participation. But such is not the case.

Because existing research lends support to the probable significance of each of the types of variables explicated by the general ISSTAL paradigm, especially where there is a reasonable amount of such research, researchers would be well advised to at least consider the possible relevance of the other types of variables in the paradigm that have been little researched for sport or outdoor recreation so far. As they have been for other kinds of social participation (see Smith & Macaulay, 1980), all the types of variables delineated by the ISSTAL Model are likely to be well worth studying in the realm of sport and outdoor recreation. The ISSTAL Model is not alone in suggesting that these various kinds of variables be studied in the present realm, though none of the other models we are aware of is quite as comprehensive as this one. Let us review some of these other models briefly here to illustrate this point.

First, it is worthwhile to recall the criticisms leveled at recreation research as summarized by Brown et al. (1973). The research done in recreation was taken to task as dealing solely with prediction without sufficient regard to understanding; it was faulted for failing to take account of a person's total life-style and for lack of development of a theoretical orientation to guide it; and it was chided for being undertaken with insufficient interdisciplinary emphasis. We would argue that the ISSTAL Model would deal adequately with all of these important problems were it to be systematically used in sport and outdoor recreation research.

As a second point, it is also worthwhile to recall the six major methodological perspectives in leisure research delineated by Burdge and Field (1972) that were described earlier in this volume. The ISSTAL Model incorporates all of these approaches. The social aggregate level is dealt with by the social background variables; the social psychological level is dealt with by personality traits and attitudinal dispositions; types of organizations are dealt with by membership status (social background and roles) and by social structure (context); activity attributes are dealt with by personality traits and by general and specific attitudes; community and regional analysis as well as social ecology analysis are dealt with by the contextual variables in the scheme. Beyond incorporating all of these divergent approaches, the ISSTAL Model as applied to the present realm also incorporates a number of other theoretical models for leisure and recreational participation that have been suggested.

Thus, Kaplan's (1975) model and all of the variables it suggests are included in the ISSTAL Model but in a manner and with terminology more consistent with the rest of social and behavioral science research and theory. Kaplan's model is artificial in having four sets of four major variable classes and not corresponding to any kind of natural process of selection or socialization. However, the ISSTAL Model has no artificiality of numerical symmetry, no neologism, and corresponds to some natural social psychological processes of selection and socialization of individuals over time as variables of increasing specificity become more and more influential for increasing degrees of participation. The ISSTAL Model also incorporates the range of variables suggested by Chapin (1974), Christensen and Yoesting (1973, 1976), Csikszentmihalyi (1975a, 1975b), Robinson (1977), and others' models. The more general model of human behavior suggested by Ajzen and Fishbein (1969) is also incorporated. These researchers argue that all behavior is essentially determined by behavioral intentions (a form of intention, in our paradigm), and that the latter is in turn determined by attitudes toward behavior in a specific situation (here "expectations"), personal normative beliefs (here "information"), social normative beliefs (here "expectations" again), and motivation to comply with social normative beliefs (here "motivational dispositions").

In addition, the ISSTAL Model deals with Burdge's (1974) comments on the problems of leisure research in general by making no value assumptions about the goodness or badness of any kind of sport or outdoor recreational participation, by being relevant to both professionals (practitioners) and researchers, and by being inherently interdisciplinary, however unpopular and risky this may be in the discipline-bound world of social and behavioral science. The ISSTAL Model is also directed precisely at the kind of future leisure research that most researchers in the field state they think should be done in the future, namely, the antecedents and consequences of leisure behavior (Crandall & Lewko, 1976). Finally, the ISSTAL Model speaks directly to the need, enunciated by Smith (1975), for metarecreation research in which the present field of study is "represented in a more formal, generalized way by projecting the phenomenon on to an external reference system" (p. 237). The ISSTAL Model transforms and synthesizes recreation research into the more general realm of social participation at large, making this kind of research a part of a larger and more abstract whole, as Goedel's Theorem indicates is necessary for increased understanding of any phenomenon. In sum, the ISSTAL Model has a lot going for it in the realm of sport and outdoor recreational participation.

There is more evidence bearing on the ISSTAL Model's value for sport and outdoor recreation research than what has just been discussed, however. In addition to providing an analytical model that incorporates prior theory and the full range of variables that have been found to affect participation and predicting that certain little-researched types of variables will have significant effects if appropriate future research is performed, the paradigm also has been generally confirmed by the small number of studies that perform multivariate analyses with different classes of explanatory variables. To start with some of the most compelling evidence, though dealing with recreational activities that are not sport or outdoor recreation, Ajzen and Fishbein (1969) tested their general model of behavior (mentioned above) on a small sample of college students. The respondents were asked about their specific attitudes ("attitudes to objects") toward eight recreational activities: attending a party, modern art exhibit, movie, concert, discussion, or poker game, or watching TV or reading a novel—all on a Friday night. For four semantic differential dimensions they were also asked their expectancies ("attitudes to acts") for satisfaction for each activity. Their personal normative beliefs (believing one should or should not do the act) and social normative beliefs (perception of friends' beliefs about whether the person should or should not do the act), which are also expectations in our model, were also measured. Then, in multiple regression analyses using behavioral intentions (stated probability of actually engaging in an activity) as the dependent variables, the authors found that approximately 70-80% of the variance could be accounted for.

In other studies it is shown that such behavior intentions in turn have a very strong association with actual behavior, so that the results in this study are important even though actual recreational behavior is not the dependent variable. The study also shows that the personal and social expectations variables (normative beliefs, in their terms) make a contribution generally to the variance explained in addition to the individual expectancies for satisfaction ("attitude to act"). And the more broad measure of specific attitude toward the various activities ("attitude to object") was moderately to strongly associated with all three kinds of expectations variables, as well as with the dependent behavior intentions variable. However, the latter association was markedly reduced when the former three expectations variables were controlled by partial correlation techniques. When this was done, specific attitudes were reduced to near zero for three activities in their association with behavioral intentions, though the remaining five partial correlations ranged from .13 to .27, with three of them being statistically significant (and in a larger sample all five would have been significant). In sum, the Ajzen and Fishbein study (replicated on other kinds of samples and dependent activity intention variables subsequently; see Fishbein & Ajzen, 1975) demonstrates rather convincingly the possible importance of the types of measures we have termed "expectations" and "specific attitudes."

Turning to more direct measures of sport or outdoor recreational activities, it is striking that the usual social status and role ("sociodemographic") variables are not very powerful in accounting for the variance in participation of individuals, even in good representative samples of the population. For instance, in a national sample with an index of outdoor recreational activity (derived from the number of mentions of participation in 11 activities), only 30% of the variance could be accounted for using mainly the standard sociodemographic variables but also including two contextual variables—region of the country and degree of urbanism of residence (ORRRC, 1962b). With another national sample of the U.S., Proctor (1962) performed multiple regressions on four major factor scores, representing types of outdoor recreation, separately for males and females in four regions of the country (thus eliminating some relevant variance associated with gender and regional context or roles). He found the variance explained to range from 4% for the backwoods activity factor among females from the South to 45% for the active recreation factor among males from the West, with most variances falling in the 10-30% range. There were major variations in the variance accounted for according to gender, region, and type of recreational activity, with the most variance accounted for in the active recreation factor, followed by the water recreation, passive recreation, and backwoods recreation factors.

Hobart (1975), with a large representative sample of the Canadian province of Alberta and using an active sport participation index as his dependent variable, found that multiple regression analyses done separately for males and females in three age categories (18-34, 35-55, and over 55 years, though the last category was not present for women) accounted for 12% to about 20% of the variance on the basis of social background variables plus a single personality measure (anomie, which we view as a personal adjustment variable). The relevance of the latter in the regression analyses lends support to the ISSTAL Model by showing that personality measures can make a significant contribution to explanation of the variance with other factors controlled. This point is shown more strongly, perhaps (though without the needed controls for other variables except in the nature of his sample), by Kane's (1970) study of students from a British university. With sport participation as a dependent variable, he accounted for about 20% of the variance among both males and females separately with the personality traits measured by Cattell's well-known 16PF inventory.

Returning to studies of more representative populations, Wippler (1968) accounted for only 14% of the variance in physically active leisure with social background variables in his sample of the province of Groningen, Netherlands. For outdoor recreation as a dependent variable, 12% of the variance was accounted for, half by social background and half by attitude variables. This shows that attitudes (in this case, general attitudes) can make a significant contribution to explaining the kind of participation of concern in the present volume. The importance of both attitude and information variables is shown by Snyder and Spreitzer (1974), though partly by omission, in their study of a representative sample of a Midwestern city in the U.S. With a broad dependent variable of sport participation (including, as noted earlier, sport participation, attending sport events, talking about sport, reading about sport, etc.), they found only about 5% of the variance could be explained with some sociodemographic variables and general attitudes regarding the meaning of work and leisure. But the zero-order correlations between the dependent variable and indices of information ("cognitive involvement") and general attitudes regarding sport ("affective involvement") are about $r = .50$, so that the variance explained if either or both of these were included in the multiple regression analysis would have to be upward of 25%. Hopefully, they will reanalyze their results in this manner sometime.

The substantial importance of social background variables beyond the usual sociodemographic ones is illustrated by the work of Christensen and Yoesting (1973, 1976). They use data gathered from a sample of adults in several Midwestern counties in a U.S. state, with the dependent variable being the use of outdoor recreation facilities during the prior 12 months. Although the usual sociodemographic variables (social status and role measures and income) are included in the multiple regression analysis, by far the most powerful variable in accounting for some 46% of the variance is one's own level of childhood activity, with the current level of one's friends' activity also being very powerful. The former is an example of an "experience and activity" variable in our scheme, and the latter is an example of the rarely used "coparticipant status" type of variable (though it might also be viewed as falling into the "information" category because it is a kind of belief about the activities of one's friends).

Curtis and Milton (1976) perform a multiple classification analysis on data from a Canadian national sample of people aged 14 years or more with dependent variables of sport activity, number of sports participated in, physical activity, and sport spectatorship. Though no explained variance figure is reported, the analysis shows that current participation in community events of various kinds (examples of "activity and experience" variables in our scheme) is significantly associated with sport participation with social background variables of the usual sort controlled. Here, too, it would be helpful if the results could be reanalyzed to indicate variance explained in a multiple regression analysis. And Hall (1973, 1976) uses a small ($n = 552$) haphazard sample of Canadian women to show that 66% of the variance can be accounted for by such key variables as present family involvement, one's own activity when younger, and age. Again, "experience and activity" variables and "coparticipant status" (or "information") are shown to be important—more important than the usual sociodemographic variables.

Only a very few studies with multivariate analyses bear on the sequential specificity aspect of the ISSTAL Model, differentiating the pattern of explanation for participants versus nonparticipants from the pattern for degree of participation among participants. The idea of sequential specificity refers not only to increasing degree of focus on a particular person's activity in a specific situation but also to the tendency for earlier and broader variable types in the model to be more important in explaining participation versus nonparticipation while the later and more specific variables are more important in explaining the degree of participation once involved (see Smith, 1966, for the demonstration of such effects in studying formal voluntary group participation). Most studies do not make a distinction between the two kinds of participation measures, either focusing on the first exclusively or combining the two.

However, Cicchetti (1972) reports extensive work he and colleagues have done with national outdoor recreation survey data from the U.S. to investigate precisely this differentiation, referring to their analysis as a "two-step" demand-supply study. The results show that the usual sociodemographic variables are the principal explanatory variables for step one, but that number of days of participation among participants is strongly affected by the relative availability and quality of recreational facilities in the individual's county or state. The latter are contextual variables, but their impact is doubtless mediated by attitudinal and information variables as suggested in the ISSTAL Model.

A more compelling example, because it includes coparticipant status as a variable, is the study by Field and O'Leary (1973), who sampled adults 18 or older from portions of three states in the Pacific Northwest of the U.S. With swimming, fishing in fresh water, power boating, and visiting a beach as their dependent variables, they report that the usual sociodemographic variables were powerful in explaining variance for participation versus nonparticipation but generally weak in explaining variance for degree of participation among participants (only 3-5% of the variance, except for fishing, which was 24%). However, the inclusion of coparticipant status variables (dummy variables regarding participation with friends, with family, or both) resulted in a marked increase in the variance explained (as much as 39% total). On the basis of chi-square analysis, Romsa and Girling (1976) find similar results for a national Canadian sample of data. Analyzing just participants in 18 different outdoor recreation activities, they find that the usual contextual (province, community size) and sociodemographic variables do not significantly distinguish people in terms of degree of participation for the 18 activities, except for walking and hiking.

Finally, the study by Murphy (1975) is the clearest evidence for the sequential specificity aspect of the ISSTAL Model in research on outdoor recreation, so far as we know. In his study of recreational boaters from the Columbus, Ohio area in the U.S., he found that 34% of the variance for his full sample could be accounted for in a multiple regression analysis of the number of boating trips people had made to a given lake during a 2-month period. What is so significant here is that the most powerful predictors were not the usual sociodemographic variables, even though these were present in the analysis, but rather the major predictors were one's specific attitude toward an alternative lake in the area, one's prior frequency of visits there, and one's travel time and specific attitudes toward the given lake. Only age, of the usual sociodemographic variables, made any significant contribution to the variance explained, and it contributed only 1%. Further multiple regression analyses with subsamples disaggregated on a socioeconomic status measure gave similar results.

There are admittedly methodological and theoretical problems with all of the just cited research, indeed with all of the research in the field. We shall note some of the most frequent of these problems shortly, but first we have a few general comments on the implications of the foregoing for the ISSTAL Model. What it all seems to add up to so far is that there clearly are differences in the pattern of explanatory variables and their power in accounting for variance in participation according to whether the measure of the latter is participation versus nonparticipation or degree of participation among participants. This is what the ISSTAL Model predicts. The paradigm also suggests that the usual contextual and sociodemographic variables will be more important for what might be called "Step 1," following Cicchetti (1972), than in "Step 2." There is evidence that this too is the case, as indicated above. Further, the paradigm suggests that among contextual and social background variables, the most important factors for explaining Step 2 participation will tend to be resources and access variables of a specific sort as well as coparticipant status and experiences and activities (insofar as one looks at specifically relevant prior or current experiences and activities). Again the evidence is consistent with this. Finally, the paradigm predicts that intellectual capacity, personality disposition, attitudinal disposition, information, and situational variables will be more important for explaining Step 2 than Step 1 participation measures. Though the evidence on this is scanty, what there is confirms the ISSTAL Model.

In summary, the available evidence on sport and outdoor recreational participation confirms not only the general relevance of the (nearly) full range of ISSTAL paradigm categories of explanatory variables, as shown earlier, but also the sequential specificity aspect of the paradigm as just discussed. No single study has yet come even close to giving the full paradigm an adequate test, however. There are always types of variables missing, either as predictors or representing the two steps of participation, and the samples involved when a broad range of variables is included are not sufficiently large or representative. Needless to say, the longitudinal aspect of the ISSTAL Model has been essentially untested in any way. For instance, the longitudinal aspect of sequential specificity predicted by the paradigm (again, see Smith, 1966) is that the usual contextual and sociodemographic variables will be more important earlier in time, filtering participants in any given kind of social participation out of the larger population. Once an individual has become a participant, the paradigm suggests, the more specific variables such as attitudinal dispositions, relevant retained information, and situational variables will be more important in explaining the degree of participation and its cessation. Personality traits and intellectual capacities will also be more important at this stage in time than earlier, insofar as they affect the fit between the requirements of the ideal participant and the nature of a particular person. Future research will hopefully shed some light on whether or not these ISSTAL paradigm predictions are true in the realm of sport and outdoor recreational participation.

## *Support for the General Activity Model*

There is also the matter of the General Activity Model and the degree of confirmation, if any, for this particular variation of the ISSTAL paradigm. It may be recalled from Smith and Macaulay (1980) that the model suggests a particular patterning of ISSTAL variables in relation to discretionary social participation. The model suggests that greater participation will be observed for individuals who have more dominant or higher, more socially valued positions in the various social status and role hierarchies of a given society. This is similar to the argument presented by Loy, McPherson, and Kenyon (1978) that the cultural system of sport supports a system of moral stratification in society where membership in preferred social categories (e.g., to be male, white, young, etc.) is associated with sport participation. In general, the research on sport and outdoor recreation confirms this prediction, finding higher participation for higher levels of education; for higher occupational prestige; for males (in our sexist society); for whites (in our racist society); for the employed; for those employed in regular "9 to 5" types of jobs (rather than in shift work, night work, or weekend work); and for those of higher social class or general prestige status in society. The results for religion, marital status, and life cycle stage are mixed. And the results for age (showing a general decline with increasing age) are apparently disconfirmatory. However, this exception can be understood as a variation of the General Activity Model: Where a particular kind of social participation is widely considered to be most appropriate for children (as in the case of sport and outdoor recreation, generally) by the people of a society, the dominant age status level for that activity will be shifted toward adolescence rather than being the usual middle-age status level, hence making participation in such activities highest for youth rather than for those in the middle years. This also accounts for the mixed marital status and life cycle stage results. Similar confounding between Protestantism and the work ethic accounts for these mixed results.

The General Activity Model predicts also that participation will be higher when there are coparticipants because doing things with others is a dominant status, and this is strongly confirmed by sport and outdoor recreation research. The model suggests that, in a similar vein, participation will be higher where the individual is a member of voluntary groups and where the person is also active in various other kinds of discretionary social participation. Again the data from the present field of participation confirm this prediction. The model indicates that participation will be higher where resources and access opportunities are greater, whether measured crudely by income or more accurately by possessions and the availability of recreational sites and facilities in the immediate environment to which one has access. Sport and outdoor recreation research strongly confirm this prediction. The syndrome model further suggests that participation will be greater where the individual has better health and high levels of psychomotor skill as well as better body condition or physical fitness. The present research review confirms this. Thus, for all of the main types of social background variables of the General Activity Model the weight of the evidence is supportive in the present research field of sport and outdoor recreation.

The General Activity Model makes predictions about psychological factors as well as social background factors. It suggests that participation will be greater for higher levels of intellectual capacities; for more socially desirable personality characteristics; for more positive attitudinal dispositions of all types (values, general attitudes, specific attitudes, expectations, and intentions); for more relevant retained information; and for situational variables favorable to participation. Although some of these types of variables have only been studied marginally (or not at all, in the case of intentions), the research reviewed in this volume generally strongly confirms the predictions of the General Activity Model just indicated. The results are rather mixed and weak for intellectual capacities and values but quite strong for personality traits, general attitudes, specific attitudes, expectations, and information, insofar as these have been studied (that is, given a variety of theoretical and methodological weaknesses of the research that has been done as limiting factors). For intentions and for situational variables, the research is so meager or nonexistent that no conclusion can be drawn.

In summary, not only does the ISSTAL paradigm in general receive significant confirmation from the research reviewed in this volume, but so does the General Activity Model variant of the broader ISSTAL paradigm. Not only are the types of variables indicated in the ISSTAL Model clearly important as predictors of sport and outdoor recreational participation with evidence of sequential specificity effects, but the directions of relationships between most of these variables and participation as indicated by the General Activity Model are generally found to hold. There are areas of exception (age, in particular) or mixed results, as well as areas of very weak, if any, research. But these do not vitiate the more general conclusion that the General Activity Model seems to apply quite well as an integrating paradigm for sport and outdoor recreation participation by individuals.

Given the fantastic welter of studies and variables studied in this field, this conclusion takes on major significance. Indeed, it argues that the General Activity Model variant of the ISSTAL Model is well worth using in future research, insofar as researchers are genuinely concerned with interdisciplinary understanding of the phenomenon of individual participation in sport and outdoor recreation. In this field, as elsewhere in social and behavioral science, many researchers are not concerned with interdisciplinary understanding. Lack of a genuine interdisciplinary interest in explaining the maximum variance possible in sport and outdoor recreation participation is the only reasonable explanation, in our view, for the continuing failure of most researchers to deal with more than one or two of the many kinds of variables of the ISSTAL Model and to perform appropriate longitudinal studies. Discipline-bound research models and paradigms dominate research on sport and outdoor recreation.

We see little hope for any rapid change in this situation, although adoption of the ISSTAL paradigm, with or without adoption of the General Activity Model variant, might induce more researchers to consider truly adequate interdisciplinary research in the present field. Adoption of the ISSTAL paradigm and General Activity Model variant of it by researchers in other fields of inquiry into social participation may encourage sport and outdoor recreation researchers to do interdisciplinary research, though again this is likely to be a very slow process. All of this may seem paradoxical because researchers in the present field, as elsewhere in the social and behavioral sciences, profess concern with the maximal advancement of knowledge regarding the phenomena they are studying. We consider this profession of concern to be partially hypocritical, whether consciously or unconsciously. There are numerous good and sufficient reasons to be found in the social structure of science for this hypocrisy—principally the discipline-bound nature of the general research paradigm used in nearly all research on individual social participation, coupled with great social structural barriers to the performance of adequate longitudinal studies (see Smith and Macaulay, 1980). Until there is a major shift from the presently dominant discipline-bound and cross-sectional study paradigm to something like the ISSTAL paradigm, sport and outdoor recreation research is unlikely to overcome such hypocrisy and move on toward truly powerful explanations of individual participation in such activities. In short, we believe that a modest Kuhnian (Kuhn, 1962) revolution is necessary in the dominant research paradigm used here, as elsewhere in discretionary social participation research, before real progress can be made in answering the critiques of the field noted earlier. But these paradigm shifts do not come easily, as Kuhn shows clearly from studying the history of science in general, and the present field of scientific research is likely to be no exception to this generalization.

## Theoretical Critique of the Literature

Having now reviewed the degree of support for the ISSTAL paradigm and its General Activity Model variant, let us turn to some criticism of existing theory and methodology in sport and outdoor recreation research. Taking the matter of theory first, it is fair to say that most research in the field is not guided by adequate theory. The closest approximation is in the realm of recreational travel studies, where gravity and inertia models, as minitheories, have been quite useful. However, these models deal with aggregated data on individual behavior, not with individual behavior per se as the dependent variable. Those models focus on the explanation of the number of visitor trips per county (or other territorial unit) to one or more recreational sites elsewhere. Aside from this small area of research, most other research tends to follow the common "shotgun approach," relating a few variables of interest to some kind of sport or recreational participation without a good theory to guide variable selection and significance testing and other analysis procedures. The discipline-bound, cross-sectional research paradigm continues to be used, with most researchers assuming that the usual sociodemographic variables will explain the most important part of the variance that is explicable. If other types of social background variables are used in a study, and particularly if personality or attitude variables are used, it is common for the investigator to ignore the relevance of the usual sociodemographic variables. The research on personality traits in relation to sport participation is an excellent example of this kind of theoretical defect.

Taking up the major variable types one at a time and commenting on the theoretical problems common in the use of each one, we consider the research performed with contextual variables to suffer from a failure to distinguish clearly between contextual roles of individuals and actual contextual effects that are related to the nature of the environment at a given point in time. This conceptual confusion is part of the more general confusion in the literature between variables characterizing the individual and variables characterizing the environment. In studying the latter, one must control for the former if the results are to be meaningful. Thus, to understand how actual variations in scenic beauty of the environment affect individuals, one must be able to measure separately and take account of individuals' perceptions of the environment, among other individual variables. The two are likely to be related, but they are conceptually different and must be treated differently methodologically if one is to approach understanding how scenic beauty affects outdoor recreational participation.

With regard to the social background types of variables, health factors are often simply ignored or sampled out (as when most studies are made of the noninstitutionalized population). Physical capacity variables seem to be important theoretically only to those researchers concerned with the performance of top athletes—not for sport and outdoor recreational participation more generally. Social status and role variables are used very commonly but almost invariably without proper regard to their true theoretical meanings for individual behavior. Thus such variables are used as proxy variables for underlying variations in role expectations that are virtually never measured directly. Hence, when social status and role variables fail to explain participation as expected, the researcher has no way of determining why this is the case. And researchers further fail to relate differential status and role expectations to differences in the full range of other psychological variables, such as motivations of other types (personality traits, values, and general and specific attitudes in particular), retained information, or intellectual capacities, or to physical characteristics of the individual, such as physical state and physical capacities.

When one considers individual experiences and activities as determinants or correlates of participation, the field has only begun to become conscious of the conceptual relevance of these variables. Earlier experiences are beginning to be studied, as noted before, but the theoretical position of prior and roughly concurrent activities is generally misunderstood. Prior activities can be used as proxy variables for prior experiences, but the fact that one is doing this should be made explicit if indeed this is what is being done. However, when one does research in this way, one is also including the confounded influence of the General Activity Pattern and the many psychological and even physical characteristics of the individual associated with it. Only by having separate measures of all of the latter kinds of variables can one use prior or concurrent activity variables as reasonable proxies for experience variables. Of course, it would be much better to measure experience more directly and to use activity measures as part of a broader set of dependent variables for analysis in studying the General Activity Pattern.

Finally, among social background variables, resources and access relationships are usually conceptualized by researchers in the present field in a very rudimentary way. By far the most common measure used is simply individual or household income, sometimes with the addition of possession of an auto. Yet the individual's resource opportunity structure is probably a crucial element in understanding sport and outdoor recreational activity, more so even than in various other kinds of social participation. Hence researchers must become more aware of the theoretical importance of environmental opportunities and limitations as factors affecting the participation of an individual if real progress toward understanding is to be made here.

In the area of more psychological variables, personality trait research is often hampered by too narrow a conception of the range of potentially relevant traits. Further, there is insufficient (indeed, virtually no) use made of the theoretical notion of personality and social status role fit or accommodation. Hence, instead of having hypotheses to guide research on which personality traits are likely to be related in which direction to sport and outdoor recreational participation (either in particular or in general), most research that troubles to use personality measures is atheoretical empiricism. It is strange, by the way, that research on outdoor recreation has virtually never considered the potential relevance of personality traits as determinants. Most of this research on personality has dealt with sport participation alone, and this usually in an organized school or professional context.

If there is a narrowness of conceptual approach in regard to personality traits, there is even more narrowness in the approach to intellectual capacities. Perhaps because sport and outdoor recreational participation seem on the surface to have so little to do with intellectual capacities, there is virtually no research on these kinds of relationships. At most we know that, in school (high school or college), athletes show some tendency to be less intelligent, but even this is contradicted elsewhere. We would argue that intellectual capacities will be found, when properly studied, to be significantly related to sport and outdoor recreational participation as to other forms of discretionary social participation.

In the realm of attitudinal dispositions, few researchers have grasped the potential theoretical importance of individual values, though research on general and specific attitudes is recently receiving increasing attention. A major problem of some of this research is the failure to relate attitudes to participation; it seems sufficient to have shown variation in leisure or recreational attitudes themselves. Theoretical confusion is also reflected in a general failure to distinguish general from specific attitudes, and both of these from either higher level individual values or lower level (more specific) expectations and intentions. Indeed, the latter two kinds of motivational dispositions virtually do not exist in the theoretical schemes of sport and outdoor recreation research, as the foregoing literature review indicates. This confusion is all part of a more general theoretical confusion in leisure and recreation research when it comes to motivation. We could find no evidence in the literature that any research had been done that viewed motivation properly (in our view) as a result of the psycho-dynamic synthesis of personality traits, values, general and specific attitudes, expectations, and intentions (see Smith & Macaulay, 1980). Hence there is not a single study that includes measures of all of these levels of motivational dispositions, or even one that includes more than three of the six levels. In all too many sport and recreation studies (and leisure studies in general), motivation is seen very crudely as the reason people give when asked why they have done or like to do something.

If one considers retained information as a kind of variable, the exist-ing research makes it clear that most researchers have no theoretical notion of the potential importance of retained information. Virtually no one has studied how such information relates to participation. This is all the more striking in view of the clear evidence that distance, competing alternatives, scenic beauty, and other aspects of sport or outdoor recreational sites have been shown in aggregate recreational travel research to be so important. There is a tendency to fail to distin-guish theoretically between motivational dispositions and retained information, assuming that the former includes all that is necessary of the latter. The first author of this volume has been guilty of this confusion in the past, for only recently has he begun to distinguish retained information as a distinct category in his ISSTAL Model (see Smith & Macaulay, 1980). There is also a tendency to fail to distinguish theoretically between context and retained information or cognition of that context. It seems to be assumed implicitly by most recreational researchers that cognition and information about the environment of an individual are perfect, so that measures of the environment can be used as nearly perfect proxies for the cognition or retained informa-tion of the individual regarding that environment when trying to under-stand participation. The work of Murphy (1975) further demonstrates that this is not the case, in the event that reflection on and perusal of the literature on sensation, perception, thought, and memory are not convincing theoretically. And Mercer's (1971b) review makes it clear that situational variables and definition of the situation are much in need of study.

Some broader theoretical failings of sport and outdoor recreation research exist as well. Only one pair of authors in the literature we were able to review seemed to begin to understand the role of the General Activity Pattern in sport and outdoor recreational participation (Curtis & Milton, 1976). Most researchers tend to ignore the theoretical importance of other kinds of discretionary social participation than the one they are most interested in studying. And if measures of other kinds of participation are included, most researchers who include such measures rather crudely consider them as predictor variables rather than as other dependent variables to be considered in conjunction with their main participation variables of interest. The reasoning for this was suggested above in discussing research on activities that are considered social background variables.

Another failing of nearly all research in the present field is failure to consider the theoretical importance of distinguishing among different types of participation variables in terms of participant versus non-participant status, degree of participation among participants, decision to participate, decision to terminate participation, and outstanding participation. The first two are usually combined, so that potentially important differences in the pattern of explanation of these two types of participation are inevitably masked. Yet some few pieces of research that have sought such differences, as described earlier, have found them as the ISSTAL Model predicts. A variation on this is the failure of most researchers to understand the theoretical importance of having reasonably representative samples of the population if research is to be cumulative and permit real growth of knowledge in this realm. If there are serious limitations in the range of population studied (as when, so frequently, school or college populations are studied because they are handy), the pattern of variables associated with participation is likely to be very different from what it would be in a more general population sample. Hence the results of such studies are non-comparable in strict terms and are likely to produce conflicting results with each other and with studies having more representative population samples. This failing is related to methodological problems, but it is a theoretical failing insofar as researchers do not understand that by dealing with a special kind of sample they are likely to produce results that are much less comparable with other studies than might be desired.

We have mentioned earlier the general failing of sport and outdoor recreation research to include more than one or two of the major categories of variables from the ISSTAL Model, a fact that shows serious theoretical limitations to be widespread in the field. However, we must also add that this same kind of narrowness of conception also affects the choice of substantive participation variables studied in the field. Quite aside from the question of degree of participation, most research in the field tends to focus on only a single type of sport or outdoor recreational participation. There have been many studies, including some national sample surveys, that have included from 10 to 20 types of participation but only very few that have tried to be relatively comprehensive. Outdoor recreation of a relatively small number of types (fishing, hunting, camping, swimming, etc.) seems to dominate the literature, with insufficient attention to sport and to other kinds of recreational activities (including indoor sport and recreation). This volume has been focused mainly on sport and outdoor recreation partly in view of our judgment that there was so little research on indoor recreation and leisure activities like hobbies and crafts that a review of that literature was not worthwhile. Yet some of the literature on "substitutability" of leisure activities, as well as the General Activity Pattern and its supporting evidence in general, suggests that a great deal more attention needs to be given to the full range of recreational activities as dependent variables and their interrelationships.

There is one area of sport and outdoor recreation research besides recreation travel where something like a minitheory has guided a significant amount of research. We are speaking here of the various hypotheses regarding the relation of work and leisure activities, as reviewed earlier in this volume under the subheading of occupational status role. These minitheories are concerned with whether leisure activity is best viewed as spillover from, compensation for, or essentially independent of the nature of one's occupational role. The results are quite mixed, as we noted earlier, and lead one to the conclusions (a) that probably all three hypotheses are true in certain circumstances, and (b) that future study should attempt to focus more on what these circumstances are, rather than simply trying to provide evidence for one hypothesis or another. In order to do the latter kind of suggested study, it will be important to include the full range of other ISSTAL variable types so that such variables can be properly controlled. At present, nearly all of the research bearing on the work-leisure relationship fails to control for other extraneous variables. Further, those interested in the work-leisure relationship should consider how this relationship may be viewed in the broader context of the General Activity Model. The latter would suggest that some of the observed relationship between work and leisure activity may be attributable to the underlying effect of psychological variables on both kinds of social participation, the one obligatory and the other discretionary. Hence, to some extent any observed work-leisure relationship may be spurious, with both kinds of participation determined by underlying psychological variables.

## Methodological Critique of the Literature

There is also much to be said on the methodological problems with the literature on sport and outdoor recreation participation. In general, the methodological level of research in the field is quite poor. There are some good, sound studies, but these are few and far between. To begin with, researchers are very often incomplete in reporting and documenting their methods. This sometimes happens when the methodology is poor in the first place.

In the area of sampling, most research in the present field is particularly bad. Much research is done with haphazard and nonrepresentative samples, with no attention to the probable biasing effects of such sampling upon reported results. Low completion rates in studies with intended representative samples further contribute to poor sampling. And in cases where the completion rate is less than, say, 90% (which is usually the case), there is very seldom any measurement of random nonrespondents in order to determine whether there are sample selection effects that may bias the results. All that is done, if anything, is to compare the respondents with normative data, usually a few common sociodemographic factors at most, that can be obtained from census figures. This is inadequate because the biasing selection effects of low completion rates may be based on psychological variables rather than social background variables, or on social background variables not included in census figures.

The widespread use of samples of high school and college students simply because they are available has already been noted. Samples of participants only for a given type of activity are also common, though the manner in which these samples are drawn makes generalization from them very risky indeed. Most frequently such user-only samples are drawn at particular recreation sites, with the relation of the particular users involved to the total population of users of a given type always left unclear. Nor is it even clear in such studies whether the particular activity sites involved in the sampling are in some way different from the average site for the given type of recreation, leaving open the possibility of major bias in the results.

Another widespread failing of the sampling in most research in the field is a small sample size. Even in the rare studies with otherwise good sampling procedures, samples are often too small to make very refined multivariate statistical analyses with any confidence in the results. Small sample size in general also contributes to the failure to find statistically significant results in a systemic way. For instance, there are several studies of personality traits in relation to sport participation that report no significant relationship to be found, although the expected trend is found in the right direction but not with enough strength to reach statistical significance in a small sample.

The tendency for researchers to sample only noninstitutionalized populations, even in otherwise well-done national sample surveys, let alone in poorer samples, has already been noted. This systematically attenuates any real effect of health on participation for the total population. Finally, in those rare national sample surveys that exist, usually with good methodology in the area of sampling except as just noted, the range of independent and dependent variables included tends to be narrow.

In regard to measurement of conceptualized variables, many additional methodological problems can be noted. One common failing is the use of subindices for a given kind of variable (for instance, general attitudes) without the use of a total index made by combining subindices. Or the reverse often also occurs, the use of a total index without corresponding use of the subindices in the analysis. Both are necessary for adequate understanding of participation. Perhaps a more common problem still is the use of very small or even single-item indices, which can only have low reliabilities. On top of this, index scale reliability coefficients are almost never reported! And, whether reliabilities are reported or not, researchers often fail to engage in adequate validation of their indices, leaving face validity as their only support.

Further, there is a widespread tendency for those researchers who use factor analysis to mistakenly create indices only for the factors that appear significant in the analysis. This is usually done by selecting the few highest loading items for the significant factors that emerge. What this does is ignore large portions of variance in the items factor analyzed because the number of factors emerging as significant seldom accounts for more than 50-60% of the total variance in the items being factored. Thus items that do not load highly on one or more of the emergent factors are ignored, even though they may be quite significant in accounting for variance in the dependent participation variable(s). Items that load highly on two or more factors are also rather systematically and unjustifiably ignored. We can find no example in the research literature where an investigator using factor analysis has not made this kind of error. There is thus a widespread methodological myth in the field that creating indices to represent the Varimax rotated factors, while leaving many other items aside, is the proper approach to measurement of conceptualized variables. This is a major error.

Still another kind of methodological failing flows directly from a conceptual failing previously mentioned: Dependent participation variables are not measured so as to analyze participation versus nonparticipation and degree of participation or outstanding participation all in the same study.

In the data collection phase of research and in general research design, most studies fail to make use of multiple methods as cross-checks on each other. There is a great overdependence on obtrusive measures to the neglect of unobtrusive measures. And in the category of obtrusive measures, self-report is by far dominant, with observation little used, even for validity checking.

In the analysis phase of research, the problems are manifold and discouraging in their implications. We have already noted above one aspect of the misuse of factor analysis by sport and recreation researchers, but there are many more as well. Perhaps the most widespread is the failure of researchers to understand the importance of or to report the results of principal components factor analyses prior to rotation to attain "simple structure" (usually by the Varimax procedure). We could find only one study (Proctor, 1962) that reported the principal components results. This means that researchers are systematically ignoring even the possibility of underlying general factors in their results and placing all their emphasis erroneously upon whatever orthogonally rotated factors emerge. With this kind of approach to factor analysis virtually uniform throughout the field (as in other areas of research as well), it is little wonder that there is little attention to the presence of a General Activity Pattern. If one will not look precisely where such a pattern is most likely to be found, if present, then one can scarcely expect to note its existence.

We suggest that if all those sport and outdoor recreational participation studies using factor analysis were reexamined, the first principal components factor in the great majority of studies would give evidence of the General Activity Pattern, as does Proctor's (1962) analysis of data from a large U.S. national sample and earlier work by the first author (Smith, 1969). What one would be looking for would be a first factor that is 2 or more times as large as the second factor (indeed, perhaps many times as large) and for factor loadings of .3 or larger for the great majority of activity items in the factor analysis. Note that such an analysis should be performed only on the activity variables, *not* with other types of variables included.

Another very common failing in the use of factor analysis in sport and outdoor recreation research is the use of a Varimax rotation of axes procedure (or some other orthogonal procedure) alone, without investigation of whether an oblique rotation procedure fits the data better. When, rarely, an oblique rotation is done, the resulting factors generally show positive covariation, again lending support to the notion of a General Activity Model (for instance, Kenyon, 1968) whether the items involved are attitudes, personality traits, participation measures, or other variables.

Other failings in the use of factor analysis in this field are the failure to report the criteria used for the termination of factor extraction or rotation and the failure to report the factor loadings of items that are loaded on several factors or that have loadings below .3. There are often important trends that can be observed from factor loadings as low as .2, and items that load highly on more than one factor can also convey substantive meaning of importance to the knowledgeable researcher. When scales are derived from factors by selection of high loading items, as is commonly done, the intercorrelations of the resulting scales (which are almost never zero, even though by definition the correlations of factor scores resulting from an orthogonal rotation must be near zero or zero) are almost never reported. This again makes it impossible to test the existence of a General Activity Pattern. Further, on those rare occasions when the factor structures from different samples are compared, the appropriate significance tests for similarity of factors are not used. And finally, although cluster analysis procedures are sometimes used as an alternative to factor analysis, these studies almost never compare the cluster and factor analytic results so that one can observe the similarities and differences in results from the two procedures. Only if both are reported can one make a reasonable determination of which is more appropriate for a given set of data, and in many cases both will be appropriate, each telling the researcher something useful but different.

In making use of significance tests there are also many failings, one of which has already been alluded to. There is a widespread tendency for researchers to fail to consider the effects of their small samples on the outcomes of significance tests. Correlations and other measures of association must be quite strong to show any statistical significance in many of the small samples that are frequently used by researchers in this field. This means that substantively meaningful relationships are ignored simply because the samples are too small for a correlation of, say, .2 to reach statistical significance. This tendency to accept the null hypothesis of no relationship erroneously is aggravated by the frequent tendency of researchers not to report significance at the .10 level as well as the .05 and .01 levels and by the almost uniform failure of recreation and leisure researchers to use one-tailed significance tests. Because one-tailed tests are by definition twice as powerful as the more usual two-tailed tests, they can rightfully be expected to show more significant results than the two-tailed tests. Of course, to use one-tailed tests of significance, one must have a hypothesis regarding the expected direction of the relationship, and sport and recreation research is, as mentioned, very weak on theory. But the ISSTAL Model's General Activity Model variant makes a whole series of predictions about the directions of relationships that will permit use of one-tailed tests. Even in those studies in the existing literature where directional hypotheses are made by the researcher, two-tailed significance tests tend to be erroneously used.

Still another failing regarding the use of significance tests is the failure to consider the attenuation of relationships that is likely to occur from nonrandom sampling and inadequate completion rates of sampling. Then, too, there is the fact that significance tests are often used with samples for which it is unclear whether the underlying statistical assumptions of the application of the test are valid, without in any way checking to see if the tests are applicable to the data in hand. Finally, there is a tendency to go too far in the opposite direction in terms of cautiousness in significance testing, with very weak statistical tests of significance used (like the familiar chi-square) when statistically more powerful tests are properly applicable.

In our view, some of the biggest failings methodologically are the general failure to use multivariate analysis procedures that permit a Proportional Reduction of Error Variance (PRE) interpretation, the failure to use controls for other major independent variable types when examining the effects of a given type of independent variable upon participation, and the failure to perform longitudinal studies with time budget-time allocation methodologies. The first failing noted means that only a tiny fraction of the research in this field permits a kind of "bottom line" determination of how well one is doing in explaining the variance in participation for a given study. This failing also relates somewhat to the second one. Multiple partial correlation or multiple classification analysis or multiple analysis of variance can all deal with the second failing without necessarily giving PRE interpretations of the variance accounted for. And the last failing is one endemic to social and behavioral science research on individuals, so it is no surprise to find it in the present field. Smith and Macaulay (1980) have discussed this failing at length elsewhere, so we will not elaborate further here. Suffice it to say that, without longitudinal and time allocation studies, we do not think much real growth in knowledge can be made in the study of sport and outdoor recreation participation from where we are now.

However, in those few studies in the literature where multiple regression analyses are used, there are still many problems that are often present. Most important of these is the problem of multi-collinearity, or the covariation of various independent variables. The effects of multicollinearity can be devastating to one's understanding of the results of a multiple regression equation. Indeed, the statistical technique of multiple regression analysis technically should not be performed if there is much multicollinearity present. But virtually no one employing the technique seems to know or care much about this. As a result, the findings from such analyses in the present field are often puzzling. These problems are exacerbated if stepwise multiple regression is the particular technique used (see Crandall, 1976).

Other problems that are common in the field in the use of multiple regression include failure to report the variance explained, failure to compare the results of a linear with a nonlinear regression analysis, failure to perform two-stage least squares regressions, failure to consider or make appropriate variable transformations prior to multiple regression analysis, failure to take account of interaction effects among predictors (which is different from the problem of multicollinearity), and failure to compute or report the variance explained after correction for the number of predictors in relation to the number of cases (or degrees of freedom). In some instances the apparently quite high amounts of variance explained are artifacts of the multiple regression procedure being performed with many predictors relative to the number of cases (for instance, Hall, 1973; Murphy, 1975). This problem is compounded by the failure of some researchers to report precisely how many predictors were entered into the regression computation, so that the reader cannot determine (in the absence of a corrected variance figure) how much of the apparent variance explanation is an artifactual result of chance.

A technique introduced in a paper many years ago (Smith & Inkeles, 1966) offers one simple solution to assessing the amount of the variance that is likely to be artifactual. One merely introduces a random number variable or a random index as a dependent variable and performs multiple regression on it with one's basic set of predictors. The nonartifactual variance in one's actual dependent participation variables of interest is then equal approximately to the observed or apparent explained variance minus the artifactual variance that is explained in the random dependent variable computation. This approach is probably more precise than the usual statistical correction for sample size and number of predictors. Finally, the present field of research makes virtually no use of path analysis in spite of the many interesting opportunities for such use that seem present. An exception is the work on socialization into sport by Kenyon (1970) and Kenyon and McPherson (1973). Whatever its failings may be, path analysis does help make sense of complex causal systems in social science research on individuals, and in our view it should be used more often in sport and outdoor recreation research. As part of such use, researchers might stop partitioning their samples by such variables as age, gender, and region of the country, introducing the latter variables in the equations involved (as dummy variables where necessary).

# *Conclusion*

To sum up, sport and outdoor recreational participation research has many inadequacies, both theoretical and methodological. These inadequacies somewhat vitiate the conclusions reached earlier regarding the degree to which the present field of research supports the ISSTAL Model and its General Activity Model variant. However, it is highly significant that the vast bulk of the research that does exist—including a small number of pieces of high quality research on national samples—confirms both models. Hence our earlier conclusions regarding both models still stand. It would be nice if future research on sport and outdoor recreation were more theoretically and methodologically adequate, so that these and other conclusions could stand on firmer ground. But this depends both on whether the models are in fact relatively accurate representations of reality and on whether sport and outdoor recreation researchers improve the quality of their research in the future, forces to the contrary (as noted in Smith & Macaulay, 1980) notwithstanding.

# References

Aalto, R. (1971). Research into how the Finn spends his leisure time. In *Sport and leisure* (Publication No. 25). Jyvaskyla, Finland: The Finnish Society for Research in Sport and Physical Education.

Aamodt, M.G., Alexander, C.J., & Kimbrough, W.W. (1982). Personality characteristics of college non-athletes and baseball, football and track team members. *Perceptual and Motor Skills, 55,* 327-330.

Adams, R.L.A. (1971). *Weather, weather information, and outdoor recreation decisions: A case study of the New England beach trip.* Unpublished doctoral dissertation, Clark University, Worcester, MA.

Ajzen, I., & Fishbein, M. (1969). The prediction of behavioral intentions in a choice situation. *Journal of Experimental Social Psychology, 5,* 400-416.

Albinson, J.G. (1971, August). *Life style of physically inactive college males.* Paper presented at the Third International Symposium on the Sociology of Sport, Waterloo, Ontario, Canada.

Aldskogius, H. (1967). Vacation house settlement in the Siljan region. *Geografiska Annaler, 49B*(2), 69-95.

Allardt, E. (1967, April). *Basic problems of comparative sociological research.* Paper presented at the International Workshop on Sociology of Sport, Urbana, IL.

Allardt, E., et al.. (1958). *Nuorison Harrastukset ja yhteison rakenne* [Youth's interests and the social structure]. Porvoo, Finland: W. Soderstrom.

Allen, L.R. (1982). The relationship between Murray's personality needs and leisure interests. *Journal of Leisure Research, 14,* 63-76.

Anderson, D.F., & Stone, G.P. (1979). A fifteen year analysis of socioeconomic strata differences in the meaning given to sport by metropolitans. In M.L. Krotee (Ed.), *The dimensions of sport sociology* (pp. 167-184). West Point, NY: Leisure Press.

Anderson, H., Bo-Jensen, A., El Kaer-Hansen, H., & Sonne, A. (1969). Sport and games in Denmark in the light of sociology. In J.W. Loy, Jr. & G.S. Kenyon (Eds.), *Sport, culture and society* (pp. 166-192). New York: Macmillan. (Original work published 1956)

Anderson, J.E. (1959). The use of time and energy. In J.E. Birren (Ed.), *Handbook of aging and the individual: Psychological and biological aspects* (pp. 769-796). Chicago: University of Chicago Press.

Andreano, R. (1965). *No joy in Mudville.* Cambridge, MA: Schenkman.

Angrist, S.S. (1967). Role constellations as a variable in women's leisure activities. *Social Forces, 45*(3), 423-431.

Aronson, E., & Carlsmith, J.M. (1962). Performance expectancy as a determinant of actual performance. *Journal of Abnormal and Social Psychology, 65*(3), 178-182.

Bacon, A.W. (1975). Leisure and the alienated worker: A critical assessment of three radical theories of work and leisure. *Journal of Leisure Research, 7*(3), 179-190.

Balog, M. (1974). The development of leisure time of married women with children in Hungary and their possibilities of acquiring further education. *Society and Leisure, 6*(1), 29-43.

Barfield, R., & Morgan, J. (1969). *Early retirement: The decision and the experience.* Ann Arbor: University of Michigan, Institute for Social Research.

Barker, M.L. (1968, August). *The perception of water quality as a factor in common attitudes and space preferences in outdoor recreation.* Paper presented at the annual meeting of the Association of American Geographers, Washington, DC.

Beaman, J. (1974). Distance and the "reaction" to distance as a function of distance. *Journal of Leisure Research, 6*(3), 220-231.

Beaman, J. (1975). Comments on the paper "The substitutability concept: Implications for recreation research and management," by Hendee & Burdge. *Journal of Leisure Research, 7*(4), 146-152.

Beaman, J. (1976). Corrections regarding the impedance of distance functions for several g(d) functions. *Journal of Leisure Research, 8*(1), 49-52.

Beamish, R. (1981). The materialist approach to sport study: An alternative prescription to the discipline's methodological malaise. *Quest, 33*(1), 55-71.

Beard, J.G., & Ragheb, M.G. (1983). Measuring leisure motivation. *Journal of Leisure Research, 15*, 219-228.

Bell, C., & Healey, P. (1973). The family and leisure. In M.A. Smith, S. Parker, & C.S. Smith (Eds.), *Leisure and society in Britain* (pp. 159-170). London: Allen Lane.

Berger, B.M. (1963). The sociology of leisure. In E.O. Smigel (Ed.), *Work and leisure* (pp. 21-40). New Haven, CT: College and University Press.

Berger, R.A., & Littlefield, D.B. (1969). Comparison between football athletes and non-athletes on personality. *Research Quarterly, 40*(4), 663-665.

Betts, J.R. (1954). The technological revolution and the rise of sport, 1850-1900. *The Mississippi Valley Historical Review, 40,* 231-256.

Betts, J.R. (1974). *America's sporting heritage: 1850-1950.* Reading, MA: Addison-Wesley.

Bevins, M.I., Bond, R.S., Corcoran, T.J., McIntosh, K.D., & McNeil, R.J. (1968). *Characteristics of hunters and fishermen in six Northeastern states* (Vermont Agricultural Experiment Station Bulletin No. 656).

Birrell, S. (1981). *The neglected half of the adolescent society: Shifts in status conferral in the high school for girls.* Unpublished manuscript, University of Iowa, Iowa City.

Bishop, D.W. (1970). Stability of the factor structure of leisure behavior: Analyses of four communities. *Journal of Leisure Research, 2,* 160-170.

Bishop, D.W., & Ikeda, M. (1970). Status and role factors in the leisure behavior of different occupations. *Sociology and Social Research, 54*(2), 190-208.

Bishop, D.W., Jeanrenaud, C., & Lawson, K. (1975). Comparison of a time diary and recall questionnaire for surveying leisure activities. *Journal of Leisure Research, 7*(1), 73-80.

Blalock, H. (1962). Occupational discrimination: Some theoretical propositions. *Social Problems, 9*(3), 240-247.

Blakelock, E. (1960). A new look at the New Leisure. *Administrative Science Quarterly, 4,* 446-467.

Bley, N., Goodman, M., Dye, D., & Harel, B. (1972). Characteristics of aged participants and non-participants in age-segregated leisure program. *Gerontologist, 12*(4), 368-370.

Boothby, J., Tungatt, M., & Townsend, A. (1981). Ceasing participation in sports activity: Reported reasons and their implications. *Journal of Leisure Research, 13*(1), 1-14.

Born, T.J. (1976a). Elderly RV campers along the lower Colorado River: A preliminary typology. *Journal of Leisure Research, 8*(4), 256-262.

Born, T.J. (1976b). Variables associated with the winter camping location of elderly recreational vehicle owners in southwestern Arizona. *Journal of Gerontology,* **31**(3), 346-351.

Bose, N.K. (1957). The effect of urbanization on work and leisure. *Man in India,* **37**, 1-9.

Boutilier, M., & SanGiovanni, L. (1983). *The sporting woman.* Champaign, IL: Human Kinetics Publishers.

Brasch, R. (1970). *How did sports begin?* New York: David McKay.

Brown, B., & Curtis, J. (1984). Does running go against the family grain? National survey results of marital status and running. In N. Theberge & P. Donnelly (Eds.), *Sport and the sociological imagination* (pp. 352-367). Fort Worth: Texas Christian University Press.

Brown, P.J., Dyer, A., & Whaley, R.S. (1975). Recreation research— So what? *Journal of Leisure Research,* **5**(1), 16-24.

Brown, R.C., Jr. (1976). A commentary on racial myths and the black athlete. In D.M. Landers (Ed.), *Social problems in athletics: Essays on the sociology of sport* (pp. 168-173). Champaign: University of Illinois Press.

Bultena, G., & Taves, M.J. (1961). Changing wilderness images and forestry policy. *Journal of Forestry,* **59**, 167-171.

Bultena, G., & Wood, V. (1970). Leisure orientation and recreational activities of retirement community residents. *Journal of Leisure Research,* **2**(1), 3-15.

Burch, W.R., Jr. (1969). The social circles of leisure: Competing explanations. *Journal of Leisure Research,* **1**(2), 125-147.

Burch, W.R., & Wenger, W.D., Jr. (1967). *The social characteristics of participants in three styles of camping* (U.S. Forest Service Research Paper PNW-48).

Burdge, R.J. (1969). Levels of occupational prestige and leisure activity. *Journal of Leisure Research,* **1**(3), 262-265.

Burdge, R.J. (1974). The state of leisure research. *Journal of Leisure Research,* **6**(4), 312-319.

Burdge, R.J., & Field, D.R. (1972). Methodological perspectives for the study of outdoor recreation. *Journal of Leisure Research,* **4**(1), 63-72.

Burns, T. (1973). Leisure in industrial society. In M.A. Smith, S. Parker, & C.S. Smith (Eds.), *Leisure and society in Britain* (pp. 40-55). London: Allen Lane.

Buse, R.C., & Enosh, N. (1977, November). Youth experience: Effect on participation in recreational activities. *Land Economics*, **53**(4), 468-486.

Butcher, J. (1983). Socialization of adolescent girls into physical activity. *Adolescence*, **XVIII**(72), 753-766.

Caillois, R. (1955). The structure and classification of games. *Diogenes*, **12**, 62-75.

Campbell, F.L. (1970). Participant observation in outdoor recreation. *Journal of Leisure Research*, **2**(4), 226-235.

Canada Fitness Survey. (1983). *Fitness and lifestyle in Canada*. Ottawa: Canada Fitness Survey.

Carls, E.G. (1969). *A study of social motives and patterns of leisure behavior*. Unpublished master's thesis, University of Illinois, Champaign.

Carls, E.G. (1974). The effects of people and man-induced conditions on preferences for outdoor recreation landscapes. *Journal of Leisure Research*, **6**(2), 113-124.

Carter, R. (1970). The myth of increasing non-work vs. work activities. *Social Problems*, **18**, 52-67.

Casher, B.B. (1977). Relationships between birth order and participation in dangerous sports. *Research Quarterly*, **48**, 33-40.

Cesario, F.J. (1975). A new method for analyzing outdoor recreation trip data. *Journal of Leisure Research*, **7**(3), 200-215.

Chapin, F.S., Jr. (1974). *Human activity patterns in the city: Things people do in time and space*. New York: Wiley and Sons.

Charlesworth, J.C. (Ed.). (1964). *Leisure in America: Blessing or curse?* Philadelphia: American Academy of Political and Social Science.

Cheek, N.H. (1971a, August). *On the sociology of leisure places: The zoological park*. Paper presented at the American Sociological Association Annual Meeting, Denver.

Cheek, N.H. (1971b).Toward a sociology of not-work. *Pacific Sociological Review*, **14**(3), 245-258.

Cheung, H.K. (1972). A day-use park visitation model. *Journal of Leisure Research*, **4**(2), 139-156.

Chipman, L.P. (1968). *A comparison of participants and nonparticipants in intercollegiate athletics with respect to selected personality traits*. Unpublished doctoral dissertation, Springfield College, Springfield, MA.

Christensen, J.E.(1972). *A sociological analysis of the high use and low use of outdoor recreation facilities.* Unpublished master's thesis, Iowa State University, Ames.

Christensen, J.E., & Yoesting, D.R. (1973). Social and attitudinal variants in high and low use of outdoor recreation facilities. *Journal of Leisure Research,* 5(2), 6-15.

Christensen, J.E., & Yoesting, D.R. (1976). Statistical and substantive implications of the use of stepwise regression to order predictors of leisure behavior. *Journal of Leisure Research,* 8(1), 59-65.

Christensen, J.E., & Yoesting, D.R. (1977). The substitutability concept: A need for further development. *Journal of Leisure Research,* 9(3), 188-207.

Chrouser, D.R. (1973). *A trend analysis of the association between leisure time physical activity participation and increase in age of male Indiana University alumni.* Unpublished doctoral dissertation, Indiana University, Bloomington.

Cicchetti, C.J. (1972). A review of the empirical analyses that have been based upon the national recreation surveys. *Journal of Leisure Research,* 4(2), 90-107.

Claeys, U. (1985). Evolution of the concept of sport and the participation/nonparticipation phenomenon. *Sociology of Sport Journal,* 2, 233-239.

Clark, R., Hendee, J., & Campbell, F. (1971). Values, behavior, and conflict in modern camping culture. *Journal of Leisure Research,* 3(2), 143-159.

Clarke, A.C. (1956). The use of leisure and its relation to levels of occupational prestige. *American Sociological Review,* 21(1), 301-307.

Clawson, M. (1964). How much leisure, now and in the future? In J.C. Charlesworth (Ed.), *Leisure in America: Blessing or curse?* (pp. 1-20). Philadelphia: American Academy of Political and Social Science.

Clayre, A. (1974). *Work and play.* London: Weidenfeld and Nicolson.

Coakley, J. (1978). *Sport in society* (3rd ed.). St. Louis: C.V. Mosby.

Coakley, J. (1986). Socialization and youth sports. In C.R. Rees and A.W. Miracle (Eds.), *Sport and social theory* (pp. 135-143). Champaign, IL: Human Kinetics Publishers.

Coleman, J.S. (1961). *The adolescent society.* New York: Free Press.

Connor, R., Johannis, T.B., & Walters, J. (1955). Family recreation in relation to role conceptions of family members. *Marriage and Family Living,* 17(4), 306-309.

Converse, P.E. (1972). Country differences in time use. In A. Szalai, P. Converse, P. Feldheim, E. Scheuch, & P. Stone (Eds.), *The use of time* (pp. 145-177). The Hague, Netherlands: Mouton.

Cottrell, F. (1961). The sources of free time. In R.W. Kleemeier (Ed.), *Aging and leisure* (pp. 55-81). New York: Oxford University Press.

Craik, K.H. (1973). Environmental psychology. In P.H. Mussen & M.R. Rosenzweig (Eds.), *Annual review of psychology* (pp. 403-422). Palo Alto, CA: Annual Reviews.

Crandall, R. (1976). On the use of stepwise regression and other statistics to estimate the relative importance of variables. *Journal of Leisure Research*, **8**(1), 53-58.

Crandall, R., & Lewko, J. (1976). Leisure research past, present, and future: Who, what, where. *Journal of Leisure Research*, **8**(3), 150-159.

Crandall, R., Altengarten, S., Nolan, M., & Dixon, J. (1977). A general bibliography of leisure publications. *Journal of Leisure Research*, **9**(1), 15-54.

Critcher, C. (1982). The historical dimension of leisure. In T. Veal, S. Parker, & F. Coalter (Eds.), *Work and leisure: Unemployment, technology and life-styles in the 1980's* (pp. 2-13). London: Leisure Studies Association.

Csikszentmihalyi, M. (1975a). *Beyond boredom and anxiety*. San Francisco: Jossey-Bass.

Csikszentmihalyi, M. (1975b). Play and intrinsic rewards. *Journal of Humanistic Psychology*, **15**(3), 41-63.

Cunningham, D.A., Montoye, H.J., Metzner, H.L., & Keller, J.B. (1968). Active leisure time activities as related to age among males in a total population. *Journal of Gerontology*, **23**, 551-556.

Cunningham, D.A., Montoye, H.J., Metzner, H.L., & Keller, J.B. (1970). Active leisure activities as related to occupation. *Journal of Leisure Research*, **2**(2), 104-111.

Curran, J., & Tunstall, J. (1973). Mass media and leisure. In M. Smith, S. Parker, & C. Smith (Eds.), *Leisure and society in Britain* (pp. 199-213). London: Allen Lane.

Curry, T.J., & Jiobu, R.M. (1984). *Sports: A social perspective*. Englewood Cliffs, NJ: Prentice-Hall.

Curtis, J.E., & Milton, B.G. (1973, April). *Social status and the active vs. sedentary societies: National data on leisure-time physical and sports activities in Canada*. Paper presented at Southern Sociological Society Annual Meetings, Atlanta.

Curtis, J.E., & Milton, B.G. (1976). Social status and the "active" society: National data on correlates of leisure-time physical and sport activities. In R.S. Gruneau & J.G. Albinson (Eds.), *Canadian sport: Sociological perspectives* (pp. 302-329). Don Mills, Ontario, Canada: Addison-Wesley.

Curtis, J.E., & White, P. (1984). Age and sport participation: Decline in participation with age or increased specialization with age? In N. Theberge & P. Donnelly (Eds.), *Sport and the sociological imagination* (pp. 273-293). Fort Worth: Texas Christian University Press.

Davey, C.P. (1975, May). *Personality and motivation of Australian participants in sport.* Paper presented at the Conference on Sport, Society and Personality, Bundoora, Australia.

Dawson, D. (1984). Phenomenological approaches to leisure research. *Recreation Research Review,* **11,** 18-23.

Deacon, J.A., Pigman, J.G., & Deen, R.C. (1972). Travel to outdoor recreation areas in Kentucky. *Journal of Leisure Research,* **4**(4), 312-331.

De Grazia, S. (1962). *Of time, work and leisure.* New York: The Twentieth Century Fund.

Di Giuseppe, R.A. (1973). Internal-external control of reinforcement and participation in team, individual, and intramural sports. *Perceptual and Motor Skills,* **36,** 33-34.

Ditton, R.B., Goodale, T.L., & Johnsen, P.K. (1975). A cluster analysis of activity, frequency and environment variables to identify water-based recreation types. *Journal of Leisure Research,* **7**(4), 282-295.

Donald, M.N., & Havighurst, R.J. (1959). The meanings of leisure. *Social Forces,* **37,** 355-360.

Douglass, P.F., & Crawford, R.W. (1964). Implementation of a comprehensive plan for the wise use of leisure. In J.C. Charlesworth (Ed.), *Leisure in America: Blessing or curse?* (pp. 30-69). Philadelphia: American Academy of Political and Social Science.

Dowell, L.J. (1967). Recreational pursuits of selected occupational groups. *Research Quarterly,* **38**(4), 719-722.

Dowell, L.J. (1973). Attitudes of parents of athletes and non-athletes toward physical activity. *Psychological Reports,* **32,** 813-814.

Dubin, R. (1956). Industrial workers' worlds. *Social Problems,* **3**(3), 131-142.

Dumazedier, J. (1967). *Towards a society of leisure.* New York: Collier-Macmillan.

Dumazedier, J. (1973). Report to a symposium on sport and age. In O. Grupe, D. Kurz, & J.M. Teipel (Eds.), *Sport in the modern world— Chances and problems* (pp. 198-199). New York: Springer-Verlag.

Dunning, E., & Sheard, K. (1979). *Barbarians, gentlemen and players.* Oxford: Martin Robertson.

Dynes, W. (1977). Leisure location and family centeredness. *Journal of Leisure Research, 9*(4), 281-290.

Edwards, H. (1969). *The revolt of the black athlete.* New York: The Free Press.

Edwards, H. (1973). *Sociology of sport.* Homewood, IL: Dorsey.

Eifermann, R.R. (1971). *Determinants of children's game styles—On free play in a "disadvantaged and an advantaged" school.* Jerusalem: The Israel Academy of Science and Humanities.

Eitzen, D.S. (1976). Sport and status in American public secondary education. *Review of Sport and Leisure, 1,* 139-155.

Engstrom, L. (1974). Physical activities during leisure time. *International Review of Sport Sociology, 9*(2), 83-102.

Etzkorn, P.K. (1964). Leisure and camping: The social meaning of a form of public recreation. *Sociology and Social Research, 49*(1), 76-89.

Eysenck, H.J., Nias, D.K., & Cox, D.N. (1982). Sport and personality. *Advances in Behaviour Research and Therapy, 4,* 1-56.

Fasting, K. (1979). *Physical activity in leisure time; factors predicting participation.* Paper presented at the Congress of Physical Education and Sport, Orebro, Sweden.

Feldman, K.A., & Newcomb, T.M. (1969). *The impact of college on students* (Vols. 1 & 2). San Francisco: Jossey-Bass.

Ferge, S. (1972). Social differentiation in leisure activity choices. In A. Szalai, P. Converse, P. Feldheim, E. Scheuch, & P. Stone (Eds.), *The use of time* (pp. 213-228). The Hague, Netherlands: Mouton.

Ferge, S., Javeau, C., & Schneider, A.P. (1972). Statistical appendix. In A. Szalai, P. Converse, P. Feldheim, E. Scheuch, & P. Stone (Eds.), *The use of time* (pp. 491-825). The Hague, Netherlands: Mouton.

Ferris, A.L. (1970). The social and personality correlates of outdoor recreation. *Annals, 389,* 46-55. American Academy of Political and Social Science.

Field, D.R. (1971). *Interchangeability of parks with other leisure settings.* Paper presented at the American Academy of Arts and Sciences Symposium, Philadelphia.

Field, D.R. (1973). The telephone interview in leisure research. *Journal of Leisure Research,* **5**(1), 51-59.

Field, D.R., & O'Leary, J.T. (1973). Social groups as a basis for assessing participation in selected water activities. *Journal of Leisure Research,* **5**, 16-25.

Fishbein, M., & Ajzen, I. (1975). *Belief, attitude, intention and behavior.* Reading, MA: Addison-Wesley.

Fisher, A.C., & Driscoll, R.G. (1975, October). Attribution of attitudes toward physical activity as a function of success. *Mouvement,* pp. 239-241.

Fletcher, R.L. (1970). *Selected personality characteristics and activity participation of male college freshman.* Unpublished doctoral dissertation, Texas A & M University, College Station.

Fletcher, R., & Dowell, L. (1971). Selected personality characteristics of high school athletes and nonathletes. *Journal of Psychology,* **77**, 39-41.

Foote, N.N. (1961). Methods for study of meaning in use of time. In R.W. Kleemeier (Ed.), *Aging and leisure* (pp. 155-176). New York: Oxford University Press.

Forer, L.K. (1969). *Birth order and life roles.* Springfield, IL: Charles C. Thomas.

Franks, C.E.S., & Macintosh, D. (1984). The evolution of federal government policies toward sport and culture in Canada: A comparison. In N. Theberge & P. Donnelly (Eds.), *Sport and the sociological imagination* (pp. 193-209). Fort Worth: Texas Christian University Press.

Freund, R.J., & Wilson, R.R. (1974). An example of a gravity model to estimate recreation travel. *Journal of Leisure Research,* **6**(3), 241-256.

Friesen, D. (1967). Academic, athletic popularity syndrome in the Canadian high school society. *Adolescence,* **3**, 39-51.

Fuchs, C.Z., & Zaichkowsky, L. (1983). Psychological characteristics of male and female bodybuilders: The iceberg profile. *Journal of Sport Behavior,* **6**, 136-145.

Gerber, E. (1974). Chronicle of participation. In E. Gerber, J. Felshin, P. Berlin, & W. Wyrick (Eds.), *The American woman in sport* (pp. 3-176). Reading, MA: Addison-Wesley.

Gerstl, J.E. (1961). Leisure, taste and occupational milieu. *Social Problems,* **9**, 56-68.

Gilliland, K. (1974). Internal vs. external locus of control and the high-level athletic competitor. *Perceptual and Motor Skills,* **39**(1), 38.

Godin, V.B., & Matz, G.J. (1976). The effect of weather conditions on back-country overnight facilities usage. *Journal of Leisure Research,* **8**(4), 307-311.

Goodale, T.L. (1965). *An analysis of leisure behavior and attitudes in selected Minneapolis census tracts.* Unpublished doctoral dissertation, University of Illinois, Urbana.

Goodspeed, C.E. (1939). *Angling in America: Its early history and literature.* Boston: Houghton-Mifflin.

Gorsuch, H.R. (1968). *The competitive athlete and the achievement motive as measured by a projective test.* Unpublished master's thesis, Pennsylvania State University, University Park.

Gould, D.R., & Landers, D.M. (1972, March). *Dangerous sport participation: A replication of Nisbett's birth order findings.* Unpublished paper presented at the North American Society for Psychology in Sports and Physical Activity, Houston, TX.

Greenberg, C. (1958). Work and leisure under industrialism. In E. Larrabee & R. Meyersohn (Eds.), *Mass leisure* (pp. 38-43). New York: Free Press of Glencoe. (Original work published in 1953)

Greendorfer, S. (1977). Role of socializing agents in female sport involvement. *Research Quarterly,* **48**, 304-310.

Greendorfer, S. (1978). Socialization into sport. In C. Oglesby (Ed.), *Women and sport from myth into reality* (pp. 115-140). Philadelphia: Lea and Febiger.

Greendorfer, S. (1979). Differences in childhood socialization influences of women involved in sport and women not involved in sport. In M. Krotee (Ed.), *Dimensions of sport sociology* (pp. 59-72). West Point, NY: Leisure Press.

Greendorfer, S. (1981). Sport and the mass media. In G. Luschen & G. Sage (Eds.), *Handbook of social science of sport* (pp. 160-180). Champaign, IL: Stipes.

Greendorfer, S. (1983). Sport and the mass media: General overview. *Arena Review,* **7**(2), 1-6.

Greendorfer, S., & Lewko, J. (1978). *Children's socialization into sport: A conceptual and empirical analysis.* Paper presented at the World Congress of Sociology, Uppsala, Sweden.

Groves, D.L., & Kahalas, H. (1975). The behavioral dimensions of free time. *Society and Leisure,* **7**(4), 135-153.

Grubb, E.A. (1975). Assembly line boredom and individual differences in recreation participation. *Journal of Leisure Research*, 7(4), 256-269.

Gruneau, R.S. (1976). Class or mass: Notes on the democratization of Canadian amateur sport. In R. Gruneau & J. Albinson (Eds.), *Canadian sport: Sociological perspectives* (pp. 108-141). Don Mills, Ontario, Canada: Addison-Wesley.

Gruneau, R.S. (1978). Conflicting standards and problems of personal action in the sociology of sport. *Quest*, **30**, 80-90.

Gruneau, R.S. (1983). *Class, sports and social development*. Amherst: University of Massachusetts Press.

Guttmann, A. (1978). *From ritual to record*. New York: Columbia University Press.

Hall, M.A. (1973, September). *Women and physical recreation: A causal analysis*. Paper presented to the Women and Sport Symposium, University of Birmingham, Birmingham, England.

Hall, M.A. (1976). Sport and physical activity in the lives of Canadian women. In R. Gruneau & J. Albinson (Eds.), *Canadian sport: Sociological perspectives* (pp. 170-199). Don Mills, Ontario, Canada: Addison-Wesley.

Hall, M.A., & Richardson, D. (1982). *Fair ball: Towards sex equality in Canadian sport*. Ottawa: Canadian Advisory Council on the Status of Women.

Hardy, S. (1982). *How Boston played*. Boston: Northeastern University Press.

Harris, D.V. (1970). Physical activity attitudes of middle-aged males. In G.S. Kenyon & T.M. Grogg (Eds.), *International Society of Sports Psychology Congress. Contemporary Psychology of Sport, Proceedings of Second International Society of Sports Psychology Congress* (pp. 419-422). Chicago: Athletic Institute.

Harris, D.V. (1973). *Involvement in sport: A somatopsychic rationale for physical activity*. Philadelphia: Lea and Febiger.

Harry, J. (1972). Socio-economic patterns of outdoor recreation use near urban areas—A comment. *Journal of Leisure Research*, 4(3), 218-219.

Hauser, P.M. (1962). Demographic and ecological changes as factors in outdoor recreation. In Outdoor Recreation Resources Review Commission, *ORRRC study report 22: Trends in American living and outdoor recreation* (pp. 27-59). Washington, DC: U.S. Government Printing Office.

Havighurst, R.J. (1957). The leisure activities of the middle aged. *American Journal of Sociology*, **62**, 152-162.

Havighurst, R.J. (1961). The nature and value of meaningful free-time activity. In R.W. Kleemeier (Ed.), *Aging and leisure* (pp. 309-344). New York: Oxford University Press.

Havighurst, R.J., & Feigenbaum, K. (1959). Leisure and life-style. *American Journal of Sociology*, **64**, 396-404.

Heberlein, T.A. (1973). Social psychological assumptions of user attitude surveys: The case of the wildernism scale. *Journal of Leisure Research*, **5**(3), 18-33.

Hecock, R. (1966). *Public beach recreation opportunities and patterns of consumption on Cape Cod.* Unpublished doctoral dissertation, Clark University, Worcester, MA.

Heinila, K. (1959). *Vapaa-aika ja urheiu: Sosiologinen tutkimos miesten vapaa-ajan kaytosta ja urheiiuharrastaksesta* [Leisure and sports: A sociological study of men's use of leisure and sports activities]. Helsinki, Finland: Porvoo.

Heinila, K. (1964). The preferences of physical activities in Finnish high schools. In E. Joki & E. Simon (Eds.), *International research in sport and physical education* (pp. 123-151). Springfield, IL: Charles C. Thomas.

Hendee, J. (1969). Rural-urban differences reflected in outdoor recreation participation. *Journal of Leisure Research*, **1**(4), 333-341.

Hendee, J., & Burdge, R.J. (1974). The substitutability concept: Implications for recreation research and management. *Journal of Leisure Research*, **6**(2), 157-162.

Hendee, J., Catton, W.R., Jr., Marlow, L.D., & Brockman, C.F. (1968). *Wilderness users in the Pacific Northwest—Their characteristics, values and management preferences* (U.S. Forest Service Research Paper, PNW-61).

Hendee, J., Gale, R.P., & Catton, W.R., Jr. (1971). A typology of outdoor recreation activity preferences. *Journal of Environmental Education*, **3**(1), 28-34.

Henderson, R. (1953). *Early American sport.* New York: Barnes.

Hendricks, J. (1971). Leisure participation as influenced by urban residence patterns. *Sociology and Social Research*, **55**, 414-428.

Hendry, L. B. (1970). Some notions on personality and sporting ability: Certain comparisons with scholastic achievement. *Quest*, **13**, 63-73.

Hendry, L.B., & Douglass, L. (1975). University students: Attainment and sport. *British Journal of Educational Psychology*, **45**, 299-306.

Henschen, K.P., Edwards, S.W., & Mathinos, L. (1982). Achievement motivation and sex-role orientation of high school female track and field athletes versus nonathletes. *Perceptual and Motor Skills, 55,* 183-187.

Hervey, J. (1944). *Racing in America, 1665-1865* (Vols. 1 & 2). New York: The Jockey Club (private printing).

Heyman, D.K., & Jeffers, F.C. (1964). A study of the relative influence of race and S.E.S. upon the activity and attitudes of a Southern population. *Journal of Gerontology, 19,* 225-229.

Hobart, C.W. (1975). Active sports participation among the young, the middle-aged and the elderly. *International Review of Sport Sociology,* 10(3-4), 27-44.

Hodges, H.M. (1964). *Social stratification: Class in America.* Cambridge, MA: Schenkman.

Hollender, J.W. (1977). Motivational dimensions of the camping experience. *Journal of Leisure Research,* 9(2), 133-141.

Huizinga, J. (1949). *Homo ludens* (R.F.C. Hull, Trans.). London: Routledge and Kegan Paul.

Husman, B. (1969, January). *Sport and personality dynamics.* Paper presented at the Annual Meeting of the National College Physical Education Association for Men, Durham, NC.

Hutchinson, B. (1972). *Locus of control and participation in intercollegiate athletics.* Unpublished doctoral dissertation, Springfield College, Springfield, MA.

Ibrahim, H. (1970). Recreation preference and temperament. *Research Quarterly,* 41(2), 145-154.

Ibrahim, H., & Morrison, N. (1976). Self-actualization and self-concept among athletes. *Research Quarterly,* 47(1), 68-79.

Ingham, A. (1979). Methodology in the sociology of sport: From symptoms of malaise to Weber for a cure. *Quest,* 31(2), 187-215.

Ingham, A., & Singh, G. (1975). The rationalization of sport. In A. Ingham, Occupational subcultures in the work world of sport. In D.W. Ball & J.W. Loy (Eds.), *Sport and social order* (pp. 344-357). Reading, MA: Addison-Wesley.

Inkeles, A., & Smith, D.H. (1974). *Becoming modern: Individual change in six developing countries.* Cambridge, MA: Harvard University Press.

Iso-Ahola, S. (1975). Leisure patterns of American and Finnish youth. *International Review of Sport Sociology,* 10(3-4), 63-81.

Iso-Ahola, S. (1980). *The social-psychology of leisure and recreation.* Dubuque, IA: Wm. C. Brown.

Jackson, R.G. (1973). A preliminary bicultural study of value orientations and leisure attitudes. *Journal of Leisure Research,* 5(4), 10-22.

Johnston, W.E., & Elsner, G.H. (1972). Variability in use among ski areas: A statistical study of the California market region. *Journal of Leisure Research,* 4(1), 43-49.

Jordan, M.L. (1963). Leisure time activities of sociologists, attorneys, and physicists, and people at large from greater Cleveland. *Sociology and Social Research,* 47(3), 290-297.

Jubenville, A. (1971). A test of differences between wilderness recreation party leaders and party members. *Journal of Leisure Research,* 3(2), 116-119.

Kando, T., & Summers, W.C. (1971). The impact of work on leisure: Toward a paradigm and research strategy. *Pacific Sociological Review,* 14, 310-327.

Kane, J.E. (1970). Report: Personality and physical abilities. In G.S. Kenyon (Ed.), *Contemporary psychology of sport* (pp. 131-141). Chicago: Athletic Institute.

Kaplan, M. (1960). *Leisure in America: A social inquiry.* New York: Wiley and Sons.

Kaplan, M. (1975). *Leisure: Theory and policy.* New York: Wiley and Sons.

Kaplan, M., & Bosserman, P. (Eds.). (1971). *Technology, human values and leisure.* Nashville, TN: Abingdon Press.

Keith, J.E., & Workman, J.P. (1975). Opportunity cost of time in demand estimates for nonmarket resources. *Journal of Leisure Research,* 7(2), 121-127.

Kelly, J.R. (1972). Work and leisure: A simplified paradigm. *Journal of Leisure Research,* 4(1), 50-62.

Kelly, J.R. (1973). Three measures of leisure activity: A note on the continued incommensurability of oranges, apples and artichokes. *Journal of Leisure Research,* 5(2), 56-65.

Kelly, J.R. (1974). Socialization toward leisure: A developmental approach. *Journal of Leisure Research,* 6, 181-193.

Kelly, J.R. (1975, April). Life styles and leisure choices. *The Family Coordinator,* pp. 185-190.

Kelly, J. R. (1977). Leisure socialization: Replication and extension. *Journal of Leisure Research,* 9, 121-132.

Kelly, J.R. (1978). Family leisure in three communities. *Journal of Leisure Research*, **10**(1), 47-60.

Kelly, J.R. (1980). Leisure and sport socialization. In D.H. Smith & J. Macaulay (Eds.), *Participation in social and political activities* (pp. 170-176). San Francisco: Jossey-Bass.

Kelly, J.R. (1982). *Leisure.* Englewood Cliffs, NJ: Prentice-Hall.

Kelly, S.L. (1969). *Personality characteristics of female high school athletes and nonparticipants in athletics.* Unpublished master's thesis, University of Iowa, Iowa City.

Kenyon, G.S. (1966). The significance of physical activity as a function of age, sex, education and socio-economic status of northern United States adults. *International Review of Sport Sociology*, **6**, 41-57.

Kenyon, G.S. (1968). A conceptual model for characterizing physical activity. *The Research Quarterly (AAPHER)*, **39**(1), 96-105.

Kenyon, G.S. (1970). The use of path analysis in sport sociology with special reference to involvement socialization. *International Review of Sport Sociology*, **5**, 191-203.

Kenyon, G.S. (1972). *Manual of the attitudes to physical activity inventory.* Ontario: University of Waterloo.

Kenyon, G.S., & McPherson, B.D. (1973). Becoming involved in physical activity and sport: A process of socialization. In G.L. Rarick (Ed.), *Physical activity, human growth and development* (pp. 304-333). New York: Academic Press.

King, J.P., & Chi, P.S.K. (1974). Personality and the athletic structure: A case study. *Human Relations*, **27**, 179-193.

Kirkcaldy, B. (1982). Personality profiles at various levels of athletic participation. *Personality and Individual Differences*, **3**, 321-326.

Kiviaho, P. (1973). Contextual analytical study about environmental effect on organizational membership and the choice of organization. *Research Reports* (No. 2). Jyvaskyla, Finland: University of Jyvaskyla, Department of Sociology and Planning for Physical Culture.

Knoop, J.C., & Kenyon, G.S. (Eds.). (1980). *International directory of leisure information resource centres.* Waterloo, Canada: Otium Publications.

Knopp, T.B. (1972). Environmental determinants of recreation behavior. *Journal of Leisure Research*, **4**(2), 129-138.

Knopp, T.B., & Tyger, J.D. (1973). A study of conflict in recreational land use: Snowmobiling vs. ski-touring. *Journal of Leisure Research*, **5**(3), 6-17.

Koehler, G.M.E. (1973). *Agents who have influenced women to participate in intercollegiate sport.* Unpublished master's thesis, Brigham Young University, Provo, Utah.

Komarovsky, M. (1967). *Blue collar marriage.* New York: Vintage.

Kreimer, A. (1977). Environmental preferences: A critical analysis of some research methodologies. *Journal of Leisure Research, 9*(2), 88-97.

Kuhl, P.H., Koch-Nielsen, I., & Westergaard, K. (1966). *Fritidsvaner I Danmark* [Leisure time activities in Denmark]. Copenhagen: Teknisk Forlag.

Kuhn, T.S. (1962). *The structure of scientific revolutions.* Chicago: University of Chicago.

Laakso, L. (1978). Characteristics of the socialization environment as the determinant of adults' sport interests in Finland. In F. Landry & W.A.R. Orban (Eds.), *Socoiology of sport: Sociological studies and administrative, economic and legal aspects of sports and leisure* (pp. 103-111). Miami, FL: Symposia Specialists.

Laakso, L. (1980). Socialization into sport involvement in Finland. In U. Simri (Ed.), *Social aspects of physical education and sport* (pp. 261-271). Netanya, Israel: Wingate Institute for Physical Education and Sport.

Landers, D.M. (1979). Birth order in the family and sport participation. In M. Krotee (Ed.), *Dimensions of sport sociology* (pp. 140-167). West Point, NY: Leisure Press.

Landtman, G. (1938). *The origin of the inequality of the social classes.* Chicago: University of Chicago Press.

Lane, C.L., Byrd, W.P., & Brantley, H. (1975). Evaluation of recreational sites. *Journal of Leisure Research, 7*(4), 296-300.

LaPage, W.F., & Ragain, D.P. (1974). Family camping trends—An eight-year panel study. *Journal of Leisure Research, 6*(2), 101-112.

Larrabee, E., & Meyersohn, R. (1958). *Mass leisure.* New York: Free Press of Glencoe.

Larson, D.L., & Spreitzer, E. (1974, May). *A sociological perspective of youth sports participation and parental involvement.* Paper presented at the Popular Culture Association Convention, Milwaukee, WI.

Lee, R.G. (1972). The social definition of outdoor recreation places. In W.R. Burch, Jr., N.H. Cheek, Jr., & L. Taylor (Eds.), *Social behavior, natural resources, and the environment* (pp. 68-84). New York: Harper and Row.

Leigh, J. (1971). *Young people and leisure.* London: Routledge and Kegan Paul.

Lentnek, B., Van Doren, C.S., & Trail, J.R. (1969). Spatial behavior in recreational boating. *Journal of Leisure Research,* 1(2), 103-124.

Lever, J. (1983). *Soccer madness.* Chicago: University of Chicago Press.

Levin, Z. (1980, December). *Intelligence of participants in sport classes.* Paper presented at the Congress of the International Committee of Health, Physical Education and Recreation, Wingate Institute for Physical Education and Sport, Tel Aviv, Israel.

Lime, D. (1969). *A spatial analysis of auto-camping in the Superior National Forest of Minnesota: Models of campground selection behavior.* Unpublished doctoral dissertation, University of Pittsburgh.

Lindsay, J.J., & Ogle, R.A. (1972). Socioeconomic patterns of outdoor recreation use near urban areas. *Journal of Leisure Research,* 4, 19-24.

Lopata, L. (1968). The structure of time and the share of physical education in the case of industrial workers and cooperative farmers in the C.S.S.R. *International Review of Sport Sociology,* 3, 17-37.

Lowenthal, M.F. (1966). Perspectives for leisure and retirement. In R. Brockbank & D. Westby-Gibson (Eds.), *Mental health in a changing community* (pp. 118-126). New York: Grune and Stratton.

Lowrey, G.A. (1969). *A mutivariate analysis of the relationship between selected leisure behavior variables and personal values.* Unpublished doctoral dissertation, University of Illinois, Urbana.

Loy, J.W. (1968). The nature of sport: A definitional effort [Monograph X]. *Quest,* 1-15.

Loy, J.W. (1976). Race and sport: A reaction to the McPherson, Madison and Landers papers. In D.M. Landers (Ed.), *Social problems in athletics: Essays in the sociology of sport* (pp. 157-167). Urbana: University of Illinois Press.

Loy, J.W., Birrell, S., & Rose, D. (1976). Attitudes held toward agonetic activities as a function of selected social identities. *Quest,* 26, 81-93.

Loy, J.W., & Donnelly, P. (1976). Need for stimulation as a factor in sport involvement. In T.E.B. Craig (Ed.), *The humanistic and mental health aspects of sports, exercise and recreation* (pp. 80-89). Chicago: American Medical Association.

Loy, J.W., & Kenyon, G.S. (Eds.). (1969). *Sport, culture and society: A reader on the sociology of sport.* New York: Macmillan.

Loy, J.W., McPherson, B.D., & Kenyon, G.S. (1978). *Sport and social systems.* Reading, MA: Addison-Wesley.

Loy, J.W., & Segrave, J.O. (1974). Research methodology in the sociology of sport. In J. Wilmore (Ed.), *Exercise and sport sciences reviews*

(Vol. 2, pp. 289-333). New York: Academic Press.

Lueptow, L.B., & Kayser, B.D. (1973). Athletic involvement, academic achievement and aspiration. *Sociological Focus*, 7(1), 24-36.

Lundberg, G., Komarovsky, M., & McInerny, J.A. (1969). *Leisure: A suburban study*. New York: Agathon Press. (Originally published in 1934)

Luschen, G. (1964). Soziologische Aspekte der Leistung [Sociological aspects of achievement]. *Allegemeine deutsche Lahrerzeitung*, 14(2) (Suppl. Leiberziehung in der Schule), 5-7.

Luschen, G. (1967). The sociology of sport. *Current Sociology*, 15(3), 1-140.

Luschen, G. (1969). Social stratification and social mobility among young sportsmen. In J.W. Loy, Jr. & G.S. Kenyon (Eds.), *Sport, culture and society* (pp. 258-276). New York: Macmillan.

Lynn, R., Phelan, J., & Kiker, V. (1969). Beliefs in internal-external control of reinforcement and participation in groups and individual sports. *Perceptual and Motor Skills*, 29, 551-553.

MacDonald, M., McGuire, C., & Havighurst, R.J. (1949). Leisure activities and the socioeconomic status of children. *American Journal of Sociology*, 54(6), 505-519.

Manchester, H. (1968). *Four centuries of sport in America, 1490-1890*. New York: B. Blom. (Originally published in 1931)

Mandell, R.D. (1984). *Sport: A cultural history*. New York: Columbia University Press.

Martindale, C.A. (1971). *Sport involvement as a function of social class and ethnic group background*. Unpublished master's thesis, University of Wisconsin, Madison.

McClelland, D.C. (1961). *The achieving society*. New York: Van Nostrand.

McEvoy, J. (1974). Hours of work and the demand for outdoor recreation. *Journal of Leisure Research*, 6(2), 125-139.

McIntosh, P.C., Dixon, J.G., Munrow, A.D., & Willetts, R.F. (1957). *Landmarks in the history of physical education*. London: Routledge.

McIntyre, T.D. (1959). *Socio-economic background of white male athletes from four selected sports at the Pennsylvania State University*. Unpublished master's thesis, Pennsylvania State University, University Park.

McKechnie, G.E. (1974). The psychological structure of leisure: Past behavior. *Journal of Leisure Research*, 6(1), 27-45.

McKillop, W. (1975). Wilderness use in California: A quantitative analysis. *Journal of Leisure Research, 7*(3), 165-178.

McKnelly, P.K. (1973). *Leisure behavior patterns: A study of residents in the lower Brazos Valley of Texas.* Unpublished doctoral dissertation, Texas A & M University, College Station.

McPherson, B.D. (1976). The black athlete: An overview and analysis. In D.M. Landers (Ed.), *Social problems in athletics: Essays in the sociology of sport* (pp. 122-150). Urbana: University of Illinois Press.

McPherson, B.D. (1978a). Aging and involvement in physical activity: A sociological perspective. In F. Landry & W. Orban (Eds.), *Physical activity and human well-being: Vol. 1* (pp. 111-128). Miami: Symposia Specialists.

McPherson, B.D. (1978b). Avoiding chaos in the sociology of sport brickyard. *Quest, 30,* 72-79.

McPherson, B.D. (1980). Socialization into and through sport. In G. Luschen & G. Sage (Eds.), *Handbook of social science of sport* (pp. 246-273). Champaign, IL: Stipes.

McPherson, B.D. (1986). Socialization theory and research: Toward a new wave of social inquiry in a sport context. In C.R. Rees & A.W. Miracle (Eds.), *Sport and social theory* (pp. 111-134). Champaign, IL: Human Kinetics Publishers.

McPherson, B.D., & Kozlik, C.A. (1979). Canadian leisure patterns by age: Disengagement, continuity or ageism. In V.W. Marshall (Ed.), *Aging in Canada: Social perspectives* (pp. 113-122). Pickering, Ontario: Fitzhenry and Whiteside.

McTeer, W., & Curtis, J. (1984). Sociological profiles of marathoners. In N. Theberge & P. Donnelly (Eds.), *Sport and the sociological imagination* (pp. 368-384). Fort Worth: Texas Christian University Press.

Meldrum, K.I. (1971). Participation in outdoor activities in selected countries in Western Europe. *Comparative Education, 7*(3), 137-142.

Mercer, D.C. (1971a, October). Discretionary travel behavior and the urban mental map. *Australian Geographical Studies, 9,* 133-143.

Mercer, D.C. (1971b). The role of perception in the recreation experience: A review and discussion. *Journal of Leisure Research, 3*(4), 261-276.

Mercer, D.C. (1973). The concept of recreational need. *Journal of Leisure Research, 5*(1), 37-50.

Meissner, M. (1971). The long arm of the job: A study of work and leisure. *Industrial Relations, 10,* 239-260.

Metcalfe, A. (1976). Organized sport and social stratification in Montreal: 1840-1901. In R. Gruneau & J. Albinson (Eds.), *Canadian sport: Sociological perspectives* (pp. 77-101). Don Mills, Canada: Addison-Wesley.

Metcalfe, A. (1978). Working class physical education in Montreal, 1860-1895. *Working Papers in the Sociological Study of Sports and Leisure*, 1(2).

Meyersohn, R. (1969). The sociology of leisure in the United States: Introduction and bibliography, 1945-65. *Journal of Leisure Research*, 1(1), 53-68.

Michelson, W. (1971). Some like it hot: Social participation and environmental use as functions of the season. *American Journal of Sociology*, 76(6), 1072-1083.

Miermans, C.G.M. (1955). *Voetbal in Nederland* [Soccer in Netherlands]. Assen, Netherlands: Van Gorcum.

Mihovilovic, M. (1973). An analysis of some factors influencing the time-budget of employed and unemployed women in Yugoslavia. *International Journal of Sociology of the Family*, 3(1), 70-85.

*Miller Lite report on American attitudes toward sports*. (1983). Milwaukee, WI: Miller Brewing Company.

Milton, B.G. (1976). *Social status and leisure-time activities* [Monograph]. Montreal: Canadian Sociology and Anthropology Association.

Moore, S. M. (1969). *Personality traits of physically active, moderately active, and inactive college women*. Unpublished master's thesis, University of Kansas, Lawrence.

Morris, G., Pasewark, R., & Schultz, J. (1972). Occupational level and participation in public recreation in a rural community. *Journal of Leisure Research*, 4(1), 25-32.

Moss, W.T., & Lamphear, S.C. (1970). Substitutability of recreational activities in meeting stated needs and drives of the visitor. *Journal of Environmental Education*, 1, 129-131.

Murphy, P.E. (1975). The role of attitude in the choice decisions of recreational boaters. *Journal of Leisure Research*, 7(3), 216-224.

Myrdal, G. (1969). *An American dilemma*. New York: Harper Torchbooks. (Originally published in 1944)

Nash, J.B. (1962). The enlarging role of voluntary leisure-time associations in outdoor recreation and education. In Outdoor Recreation Resources Review Commission, *ORRRC report no. 22: Trends in American living and outdoor recreation* (pp. 157-186). Washington, DC: U.S. Government Printing Office.

National Recreation Association. (1934). *The leisure hours of 5,000 people.* New York: Author.

Neulinger, J. (1974). *The psychology of leisure.* Springfield, IL: Charles C. Thomas.

Neulinger, J., & Breit, M. (1969). Attitude dimensions of leisure. *Journal of Leisure Research, 1*(3), 255-261.

Neulinger, J., & Breit, M. (1971). Attitude dimensions of leisure: A replication study. *Journal of Leisure Research, 3*(2), 108-115.

Neulinger, J., Light, S., & Mobley, T. (1976). Attitude dimensions of leisure in a student population. *Journal of Leisure Research, 8*(3), 175-176.

Niblock, N.W. (1967). *Personality traits and intelligence level of female athletes and nonparticipants from McNally High School.* Unpublished master's thesis, University of Washington, Seattle.

Nicosia, F.M. (1966). *Consumer decision processes: Marketing and advertising implications.* Englewood Cliffs, NJ: Prentice-Hall.

Nielson, J. (1969). *Toward a sociological theory of forest recreation.* Unpublished master's thesis, Institute for Sociological Research, University of Washington, Seattle.

Nielson, J., & Catton, W. (1971). Forest recreation propositional inventory. *Journal of Leisure Research, 3*(3), 178-193.

Nisbett, R.E. (1968). Birth order and participation in dangerous sports. *Journal of Personality and Social Psychology, 8*(4), 351-353.

Nix, J.B. (1969). *Motivational reasons for participation and nonparticipation in inter-scholastic athletics.* Unpublished master's thesis, Sacramento State College.

Nixon, H.L., II. (1984a). The creation of appropriate integration opportunities in sport for disabled and nondisabled people: A guide for research and action. *Sociology of Sport Journal, 1*, 184-192.

Nixon, H.L., II. (1984b). Handicapism and sport: New directions for sport sociology research. In N. Theberge & P. Donnelly (Eds.), *Sport and the sociological imagination* (pp. 162-176). Fort Worth: Texas Christian University Press.

Noe, F.P. (1971). Autonomous spheres of leisure activity for the industrial executive and blue collarite. *Journal of Leisure Research, 3*(4), 220-249.

Norwegian Confederation of Sport. (1984). *Physical activity in Norway, 1983.* Oslo: Norwegian Confederation of Sport.

Nye, F.I. (1958). Employment status and recreational behavior of mothers. *Pacific Sociological Review*, **1**, 69-72.

O'Connor, C.A. (1970). *A study of personality needs involved in the selection of specific leisure interest groups.* Unpublished doctoral dissertation, University of Southern California, Los Angeles.

Ogilvie, B.C. (1974). The sweet psychic jolt of danger. *Psychology Today*, **8**(5), 88-94.

Oglesby, C. (1978). The masculinity/feminity game: Called on account of. In C. Oglesby (Ed.), *Women and sport: From myth to reality* (pp. 75-88). Philadelphia: Lea and Febiger.

O'Leary, J.T., Field, D.R., & Schreuder, G. (1974). Social groups and water activity clusters: An exploration of interchangeability and substitution. In D.R. Field, J.C. Barron, & F. Long (Eds.), *Water and community development: Social and economic perspectives* (pp. 195-215). Ann Arbor, MI: Science Publishing.

*Ontario Recreation Survey.* (1977). Toronto, Ontario: Resources Development Secretariat.

Orlick, T.D. (1973). An analysis of expectancy as a motivational factor influencing sports participation. *International Society of Sports Psychology, Third World Congress. Proceedings: Vol. 2* (pp. 1-8). Madrid: Institute Nacional de Educacion Fisica y Deportes.

Orlick, T.D. (1974). Sport participation—A process of shaping behavior. *Human Factors*, **16**(5), 558-561.

Orlick, T.D. (1980). Cooperative play and games. In J. Knight (Ed.), *All about play: A handbook of resources on children's play.* Ottawa: Canadian Council on Children and Youth.

Orlick, T.D., & Botterill, C. (1979). *Every kid can win.* Chicago: Nelson-Hall.

O'Rourke, B. (1974). Travel in the recreational experience—A literature review. *Journal of Leisure Research*, **6**, 140-156.

Orthner, D.K. (1975). Leisure activity patterns and marital satisfaction over the marital career. *Journal of Marriage and the Family*, **37**(1), 91-104.

Orthner, D.K. (1976). Patterns of leisure and marital interaction. *Journal of Leisure Research*, **8**(2), 98-111.

Otto, L.B., & Alwin, D.F. (1977). Athletics, aspirations and attainments. *Sociology of Education*, **50**(2), 102-113.

Outdoor Recreation Resource Review Commission. (1962a). *National recreation survey, ORRRC study report no. 19.* Washington, DC: U.S. Government Printing Office.

Outdoor Recreation Resource Review Commission. (1962b). *Participation in outdoor recreation: Factors affecting demand among American adults. ORRRC study report no. 20.* Washington, DC: U.S. Government Printing Office.

Outdoor Recreation Resource Review Commission. (1962c). *Trends in American living and outdoor recreation. ORRRC study report no. 22.* Washington, DC: U.S. Government Printing Office.

Owen, J.D. (1969). *The price of leisure: An economic analysis of the demand for leisure time.* Rotterdam, Netherlands: Rotterdam University Press.

Owen, J.D. (1971). The demand for leisure. *Journal of Political Economy,* **79**(1), 56-76.

Pacey, P.L. (1982). Equal opportunity for women in intercollegiate sports: Financial aid and family background as major influences on female participation in competitive programs. *American Journal of Economics and Sociology,* **41**, 257-268.

Page, C. (1973). The world of sport and its study. In J. Talamini & C. Page (Eds.), *Sport and society* (pp. 1-39). Boston: Little, Brown.

Parker, S. (1971). *The future of work and leisure.* New York: Praeger.

Pearson, J.W. (1973). *The 8 day week.* New York: Harper & Row.

Peirce, C.H. (1975). Recreation for the elderly: Activity participation at a senior citizen center. *Gerontologist,* **15**(3), 202-205.

*Physical activity patterns in Ontario.* (1981). Toronto: Ontario Ministry of Culture and Recreation.

Pooley, J. (1981). *Drop-outs from sport: A case study of boys age group soccer.* Paper presented at the American Alliance for Health, Physical Education, Recreation and Dance Convention, Boston.

Poor, R. (1970). *4 days, 40 hours.* Cambridge, MA: Bursk and Poor.

Proctor, C. (1962). Dependence of recreation participation on background characteristics of sample persons in the September 1960 National Recreation Survey. In Outdoor Resources Recreation Review Commission, *ORRRC study report no. 19* (pp. 77-94). Washington, DC: U.S. Government Printing Office.

Pudelkiewicz, E. (1970). Sociological problems of sports in housing estates. *International Review of Sport Sociology,* **5**, 73-103.

Rader, B.G. (1983). *American sports: From the age of folk games to the age of spectators.* Englewood Cliffs, NJ: Prentice-Hall.

Ragheb, M.G., & Beard, J.G. (1982). Measuring leisure attitude. *Journal of Leisure Research,* **14**, 155-167.

Rapoport, R., & Rapoport, R.N. (1975). *Leisure and the family life cycle.* London: Routledge and Kegan Paul.

Rehberg, R.A., & Cohen, M. (1976). Political attitudes and participation in extracurricular activities. In D.M. Landers (Ed.), *Social problems in athletics* (pp. 201-211). Urbana: University of Illinois Press.

Reich, C.M. (1965). *Socioeconomic factors related to household participation in community recreation.* Unpublished doctoral dissertation, Pennsylvania State University, University Park.

Riesman, D. (1958). Leisure and work in post-industrial society. In E. Larrabee & R. Meyersohn (Eds.), *Mass leisure* (pp. 363-385). New York: Free Press of Glencoe.

Riesman, D., & Denny, R. (1954). Football in America. In D. Riesman (Ed.), *Individualism reconsidered* (pp. 242-257). New York: Free Press of Glencoe.

Riiskjar, S. (1984, July). *Participation in different forms of sport among the adult population—Toward new participation structures in sport.* Paper presented at the Olympic Scientific Congress, Eugene, Oregon.

Rijsdorp, K. (1960). *Sports als john-menseliijke activiteit* [Sport as activity of youth]. Groningen, Netherlands: Wolters.

Riordan, J. (1977). *Sport in Soviet society.* Cambridge: Cambridge University Press.

Riordan, J. (1980). *Soviet sport.* Oxford: Basil Blackwell.

Ritchie, J.R.B. (1975). On the derivation of leisure activity types— A perceptual mapping approach. *Journal of Leisure Research, 7*(2), 128-140.

Roberts, J.M., Arth, M.J., & Bush, R.R. (1959). Games in culture. *American Anthropologist, 61*(4), 597-605.

Roberts, J.M., & Sutton-Smith, B. (1962). Child training and game involvement. *Ethnology, 1*(2), 166-185.

Roberts, K. (1978). *Contemporary society and the growth of leisure.* London: Longman.

Robinson, J.P. (1967). Time expenditures on sports across ten countries. *International Review of Sport Sociology, 2*, 67-84.

Robinson, J.P. (1969). Social change as measured by time budgets. *Journal of Leisure Research, 1*(1), 75-77.

Robinson, J.P. (1977). *How Americans use time: A social-psychological analysis of everyday behavior.* New York: Praeger.

Robinson, J.P., & Converse, P.E. (1972). Social change reflected in the use of time. In A. Campbell & P. Converse (Eds.), *The human meaning of social change* (pp. 17-86). New York: Russell Sage Foundation.

Robinson, J.P., Converse, P.E., & Szalai, A. (1972). Everyday life in twelve countries. In A. Szalai, P. Converse, P. Feldheim, E. Scheuch, & P. Stone (Eds.), *The use of time* (pp. 113-144). The Hague, Netherlands: Mouton.

Rogers, R. (1974). Normative aspects of leisure time behavior in the Soviet Union. *Sociology and Social Research, 58*(4), 369-379.

Romsa, G.H. (1973). A method of deriving outdoor recreational activity packages. *Journal of Leisure Research, 5*(4), 34-46.

Romsa, G.H., & Girling, S. (1976). The identification of outdoor recreation market segments on the basis of frequency of participation. *Journal of Leisure Research, 8*(4), 247-255.

Sage, G. (1980). Sport and religion. In G. Luschen & G. Sage (Eds.), *Handbook of social science of sport* (pp. 147-159). Champaign, IL: Stipes.

Salaman, G. (1974). *Community and occupation: An exploration of work/leisure relationships.* London: Cambridge University Press.

Scheuch, E.K. (1960). Family cohesion and leisure time. *Sociological Review, 8*, 37-61.

Schmitz-Scherzer, R., Rudinger, R., Angleitner, A., & Bierhoff-Alfermann, D. (1974). Note on a factor-analysis comparative study of leisure activities in four different samples. *Journal of Leisure Research, 6*(1), 77-83.

Seneca, J.J., Davidson, P., & Adams, F.G. (1968). An analysis of recreation use of the TVA Lakes. *Land Economics, 4*(4), 529-534.

Senters, J.M. (1971). A function of uncertainty and stakes in recreation. *Pacific Sociological Review, 14*(3), 259-269.

Seppanen, P. (1981). Olympic success: A cross-cultural perspective. In G. Luschen & G. Sage (Eds.), *Handbook of social science of sport* (pp. 93-116). Champaign, IL: Stipes.

Sessoms, H.D. (1963). An analysis of the selected variables affecting outdoor recreational patterns. *Social Forces, 42*(1), 112-115.

Sessoms, H.D., & Oakley, S.R. (1969). Recreation, leisure and the alcoholic. *Journal of Leisure Research, 1*(1), 21-32.

Shafer, E.L., Hamilton, J.F., & Schmidt, E.A. (1969). Natural landscape preferences: A predictive model. *Journal of Leisure Research, 1*(1), 1-19.

Shafer, E.L., & Tooby, M. (1972). Landscape preferences: An international replication. *Journal of Leisure Research, 5*(3), 60-63.

Shepard, J.M. (1974). A status recognition model of work-leisure relationships. *Journal of Leisure Research, 6*(1), 58-63.

Sillitoe, K.K. (1967). *The pilot national recreation study. Report No. 1.* Keele, England: The University Press and the British Travel Association.

Sillitoe, K.K. (1969). *Planning for leisure.* London: Governmental Social Survey, Her Majesty's Stationery Office.

Slusher, H.S. (1964). Personality and intelligence characteristics of selected high school athletes and nonathletes. *Research Quarterly (AAHPER), 35*, 539-545.

Smith, D.H. (1966). A psychological model of individual participation in formal voluntary organizations: Application to some Chilean data. *American Journal of Sociology, 72*, 249-266.

Smith, D.H. (1969, August). Evidence for a general activity syndrome. In E. Mallenoff & P. Walsh (Eds.), *Proceedings of the American Psychological Association 77th Annual Convention* (pp. 453-454). Washington, DC: American Psychological Association.

Smith, D.H. (1975). Voluntary action and voluntary groups. In A. Inkeles, J. Coleman, & N. Smelser (Eds.), *Annual review of sociology: Vol. 1* (pp. 247-270). Palo Alto, CA: Annual Reviews.

Smith, D.H. (1980). Methods of inquiry and theoretical perspectives. In D.H. Smith & J. Macaulay (Eds.), *Participation in social and political activities.* San Francisco: Jossey-Bass.

Smith, D.H., & Inkeles, A. (1966). The OM Scale: A comparative sociopsychological measure of individual modernity. *Sociometry, 29,* 353-377.

Smith, D.H., & Macaulay, J. (1980). *Participation in social and political activities.* San Francisco: Jossey-Bass.

Smith, M.A., Parker, S., & Smith, C.S. (Eds.). (1973). *Leisure and society in Britain.* London: Allen Lane.

Smith, M.D. (1979). Getting involved in sport: Sex differences. *International Review of Sport Sociology, 14,* 93-101.

Snyder, E.E. (1969). A longitudinal analysis of the relationship between high school student values, social participation, and educational-occupational achievement. *Sociology of Education, 42,* 261-270.

Snyder, E.E., & Kivlin, J.E. (1975). Women athletes and aspects of psychological well-being and body image. *Research Quarterly (AAHPER), 46*(2), 191-199.

Snyder, E.E., & Spreitzer, E.A. (1973). Family influence and involvement in sports. *Research Quarterly*, **44**(3).

Snyder, E.E., & Spreitzer, E.A. (1974). Orientations toward work and leisure as predictors of sports involvement. *Research Quarterly*, **45**(4), 398-406.

Snyder, E.E., & Spreitzer, E.A. (1976). Correlates of sport participation among adolescent girls. *Research Quarterly*, **47**(4), 804-809.

Snyder, E.E., & Spreitzer, E.A. (1978). Socialization comparisons of adolescent female athletes and musicians. *Research Quarterly*, **49**(3), 342-350.

Snyder, E.E., Spreitzer, E., & Kivlin, J. (1975). *Attitudes toward female participation in sport.* Unpublished manuscript, Bowling Green State University, Department of Sociology, Bowling Green, OH.

Sofranko, A.J., & Nolan, M.F. (1972). Early life experiences and adult sports participation. *Journal of Leisure Research*, **4**(1), 6-18.

Sonnenfeld, J. (1966). Variable values in space landscape: An inquiry into the nature of environmental necessity. *Journal of Social Issues*, **22**(4), 71-82.

Soule, G. (1957). The economics of leisure. In P.F. Douglass (Ed.), *Recreation in the age of automation. Annals of the American Academy of Political and Social Science* (No. 313, pp. 16-24). Philadelphia, PA: The American Academy of Political and Social Science.

Spreitzer, E., & Snyder, E. (1983). Correlates of participation in adult recreation sports. *Journal of Leisure Research*, **15**(1), 27-38.

Standlee, L.S., & Popham, W.J. (1958). Participation in leisure time activities as related to selected vocational and social variables. *Journal of Psychology*, **46**, 149-154.

Statistics Canada. (1978). *Culture statistics: Recreational activities.* Ottawa: Author.

Stebbins, C. (1969). *Achievement in sport as a function of personality and social situation.* Unpublished master's thesis, University of Wisconsin, Madison.

Stebbins, R. (1979). *Amateurs.* Beverly Hills, CA: Sage.

Steele, P.D., & Zurcher, L.A., Jr. (1973). Leisure sports as ephemeral roles: An exploratory study. *Pacific Sociological Review*, **16**(3), 345-356.

Steiner, J.F. (1970). *Americans at play.* New York: Arno Press. (Originally published in 1933)

Stensaasen, S. (1974). School sport on a voluntary basis. *International Review of Sport Sociology, 9*(3-4), 33-44.

Stockfelt, T. (1970). Psychological analyses of Swedish elite athletes. In G. Kenyon (Ed.), *Contemporary psychology of sport* (pp. 217-223). Chicago: The Athletic Institute.

Stockman, P. (1974). More leisure for employed mothers. *Society and Leisure, 26*(1), 141-153.

Stone, G.P. (1957). Some meanings of American sport. *Proceedings of the 60th annual meeting of the College Physical Education Association* (pp. 6-29). Columbus, OH.

Stone, G.P. (1968). Some meanings of American sport: An extended view. In G.S. Kenyon (Ed.), *Aspects of contemporary sport sociology* (pp. 5-16). Chicago: The Athletic Institute.

Stotland, E., Sherman, S.E., & Shaver, K.G. (1971). *Empathy and birth order.* Lincoln: University of Nebraska Press.

Strzeminska, H. (1972). Educational status and time budgets. In A. Szalai, P. Converse, P. Feldheim, E. Scheuch, & P. Stone (Eds.), *The use of time* (pp. 377-395). The Hague, Netherlands: Mouton.

Sutton-Smith, B. (1953). Marbles are in. *Western Folklore, 121*(3), 186-193.

Sutton-Smith, B., Roberts, J., & Kozelka, R. (1963). Game involvement in adults. *Journal of Social Psychology, 60*, 15-30.

Sutton-Smith, B., & Rosenberg, B.G. (1961). Sixty years of historical change in the game preferences of American children. *Journal of American Folklore, 74*(1), 17-46.

Szalai, A., Converse, P., Feldheim, P., Scheuch, E., & Stone, P. (Eds.). (1972). *The use of time.* The Hague, Netherlands: Mouton.

Talamini, J.T., & Page, C.H. (Eds.). (1973). *Sport and society: An anthology.* Boston: Little, Brown.

Tatham, R.L., & Dornoff, R.J. (1971). Market segmentation for outdoor recreation research. *Journal of Leisure Research, 3*, 5-16.

Taylor, C.E., & Knudson, D.M. (1973). Area preferences of Midwestern campers. *Journal of Leisure Research, 5*, 39-48.

Thayer, R.L., Hodgson, R.W., Gustke, L.D., Atwood, B.G., & Holmes, J. (1976). Validation of a natural landscape preference model as a predictor of perceived landscape beauty in photographs. *Journal of Leisure Research, 8*(4), 292-299.

Theberge, N., Curtis, J., & Brown, B. (1982). Sex differences in orientations toward games: Tests of the sport involvement hypothesis.

In A. Dunleavy, A. Miracle, & C. R. Rees (Eds.), *Studies in the sociology of sport* (pp. 285-308). Fort Worth: Texas Christian University Press.

Thirer, J., & Wright, S.D. (1985). Sport and social status for adolescent males and females. *Sociology of Sport Journal, 2*, 164-171.

Thomas, L.C. (1956). Leisure pursuits by socioeconomic status. *Journal of Educational Sociology, 29*, 367-377.

Tinsley, H.E.A., Barrett, J.C., & Kass, R.A. (1977). Leisure activities and need satisfaction. *Journal of Leisure Research, 9*(2), 110-120.

Torbert, W.R., & Rogers, M.P. (1973). *Being for the most part puppets: Interactions among men's labor, leisure, and politics.* Cambridge, MA: Schenkman.

Treble, G., & Neil, J. (1972). Folklore and women's participation in sports. *Australia Journal of Physical Education, 55*, 38-41.

Tuan, Y. (1974). *Topophilia. A study of environmental perception, attitudes and values.* Englewood Cliffs, NJ: Prentice-Hall.

Unkel, M. (1981). Physical recreation participation of females and males during the adult life cycle. *Leisure Sciences, 4*, 1-27.

Van der Smissen, B., & Joyce, D.V. (1970). *Bibliography of theses and dissertations in recreation, parks, camping and outdoor education.* Washington, DC: National Recreation and Park Association.

Vander Velden, L. (1971, March). *Birth order, family size, male siblings and athletic participation.* Paper presented in the research section of the Annual Meeting of the American Association of Health, Physical Education and Recreation, Detroit.

Vaux, H.J. (1975). The distribution of income among wilderness users. *Journal of Leisure Research, 7*(1), 29-37.

Veal, A.J. (1982). *Work/leisure relationships: A closer look.* Paper presented at the Tenth World Congress of the International Sociological Association, meeting of the Research Committee on Leisure, Mexico City.

Veblen, T. (1899). *Theory of the leisure class.* New York: Macmillan.

Wade, S. (1973). Interpersonal discussion: A critical predictor of leisure study. *Journal of Communication, 23*(4), 429-441.

Wagner, F.W., & Donohue, T.R. (1976). The impact of inflation and recession on urban leisure in New Orleans. *Journal of Leisure Research, 8*(4), 300-306.

Warburton, F.W., & Kane, J.E. (1966). Personality correlates of sport and physical abilities. In J.E. Kane (Ed.), *Readings in physical edu-*

*cation* (pp. 61-89). London: Physical Education Association.

Ward, E., Hardman, K., & Almond, L. (n.d.). *Investigation into the pattern of participation in physical activity of 11 to 18 year old boys.* North West Counties Physical Education Association.

Weaver, R.B. (1968). *Amusements and sports in American life.* Westport, CT: Greenwood Press. (Originally published in 1939)

White, R.C. (1955). Social class differences in the use of leisure. *American Journal of Sociology,* **61,** 145-150.

White, T.H. (1975). The relative importance of education and income as predictors in outdoor recreation participation. *Journal of Leisure Research,* **7**(3), 191-199.

Whitson, D. (1978). *Research methodology in sport sociology* [Monograph]. Ottawa: Canadian Association for Health, Physical Education and Recreation.

Wilensky, H.L. (1961). The uneven distribution of leisure: The impact of economic growth on "free time." *Social Problems,* **9,** 32-56.

Wilkinson, P.F. (1973). The use of models in predicting the consumption of outdoor recreation. *Journal of Leisure Research,* **5**(3), 34-48.

Williams, R.M. (1970). *American society.* New York: Knopf.

Willmott, P. (1971). Family, work and leisure conflicts among male employees. *Human Relations,* **24**(6), 575-584.

Winter, D.G. (1973). *The power motive.* New York: The Free Press.

Wippler, R. (1968). *Sociale determinaten het vrijetijdsgedrag* [Social determinants of leisure behavior]. Groningen, Netherlands: Van Gorcum.

Witt, P.A. (1971). Factor structure of leisure behavior for high school age youth in three communities. *Journal of Leisure Research,* **3,** 213-219.

Witt, P.A., & Bishop, D.W. (1970). Situational antecedents to leisure behavior. *Journal of Leisure Research,* **2**(1), 64-77.

Wohl, A. (1969). Engagement in sports activity on the part of workers of large industrial establishments in People's Poland. *International Review of Sport Sociology,* **4,** 83-127.

Wolfe, R.I. (1972). The inertia model. *Journal of Leisure Research,* **4**(1), 73-76.

Wolfenstein, M. (1958). The emergence of fun morality. In E. Larrabee & R. Meyersohn (Eds.), *Mass leisure* (pp. 86-96). New York: Free Press. (Originally published in 1951)

Wonneberger, I. (1968). The role of physical culture and sport in leisure pursuits of women as compared with that of men. *International Review of Sport Sociology,* **3,** 116-124.

Wyrick, W. (1974). Biophysical perspectives. In E. Gerber, J. Felshin, P. Berlin, & W. Wyrick (Eds.), *The American woman in sport* (pp. 401-529). Reading, MA: Addison-Wesley.

Yancey, W.L., & Snell, J. (1971, December). *Parks as aspects of leisure in the innercity: An exploratory investigation.* Paper presented at the AAAS Symposium, Philadelphia, PA.

Yiannakis, A. (1976). Birth order and preference for dangerous sports among males. *Research Quarterly,* **47**(1), 62-67.

Yoesting, D.R., & Burkhead, D.L. (1973). Significance of childhood recreation experience on adult leisure behavior: An exploratory analysis. *Journal of Leisure Research,* **5**(1), 25-36.

Zeisel, J. (1958). The workweek in American industry 1850-1956. In E. Larrabee & R. Meyersohn (Eds.), *Mass leisure* (pp. 145-153). New York: Free Press.

Zurn, M. (1971). Sport and physical recreation in the leisure time culture of big town dwellers. *Society and Leisure,* **3,** 149-157.

# Index

## A

Achievement
    as cultural value, 16, 17
    need for, 92
Action space, 76
Age, 33-37, 51, 100, 126
    and General Activity Model, 129
Altruism, 87
"American sports creed," 115
Assertiveness, 87
Attitude scales, 98
Attitudes, 93, 96-97, 103, 133-134
    and General Activity Model, 129
    and ISSTAL Model, 121-127
    measurement, 97-98
    toward camping, 102-104, 113, 116
    toward environmental issues, 99
    toward jobs and work, 100
    toward leisure, 78
    toward outdoors, 99
    toward physical activity, 97
    toward sites for activities, 104-105
    toward sport and outdoor recreation (general), 96-100
Automobiles, 65-66
"Awareness space," 76-77, 113

## B

Beliefs, and ISSTAL Model, 121, 122
Biophysical environmental variables, 10-13
Birth order, 30-31
Blacks, 37-39. *See also* Race
    perception of wilderness areas, 113

## C

## D

## E

Intelligence, 83-84
  and General Activity Model, 129
  and intellectual orientations, 94
  and ISSTAL Model, 127
  study of, 133
Intentions
  and General Activity Model, 129
  and ISSTAL Model, 14, 120, 121-123
  study of, 134
ISSTAL Model (Interdisciplinary Sequential Specificity Time
      Allocation Lifespan), 6, 90, 107, 119, 143
  and General Activity Model, 129-131
  and study of sport and outdoor recreational participation,
      120-128, 134, 135

**L**

Leisure
  defined, 2
  study of, 1, 4-6, 121

**M**

Marital status, 47-49
  interaction with employment status, 48
  and running, 49
Media
  climatic variation, 11
  consumption of, as leisure, 20-21
  TV viewing, 67
Membership in voluntary groups, 71-72
  and General Activity Model, 129
Mental health, 29
Motivations
  for general sport and recreational participation, 95, 96
  and ISSTAL Model, 121
  for specific sport and recreational participation, 101-103
  study of, 133

**N**

Nationality, 53
Need for achievement, 92

# O

Occupation structure, 20
Occupational prestige, 59-63. *See also* Socioeconomic status
   and General Activity Model, 128
Occupational role, 67-69
Opportunity for recreational participation, 12-13, 64-67

# P

Personality traits, 84-92
   and General Activity Model, 129
   and ISSTAL Model, 124, 127
   study of, 89-90, 133-134
Physiological factors, 26-28
   and General Activity Model, 129
   study of, 132
Play, 2-3, 108
Prestige, rankings of sport and recreational activities by, 14-16
Prominence, need for, 87-92

# R

Race, 37-39
   and General Activity Model, 128
Recreation
   defined, 2-4
   research on, 120-121
Religion, 17, 39-40
Residence, 11-12, 23-24. *See also* Geographic roles
Resource opportunity structure, 21, 133
Resources and access factors, 63-67, 129, 132-133
Retained information, 111-115
   and General Activity Model, 129
   study of, 134
Retirement, 46, 82
Rural-urban factors affecting leisure, 23-24
Rural-urban residence, 11

# S

Seasonal variations. *See* Climate and social participation
Selection vs. social learning effects, 90
Self-actualization, 88

# W

Weather. *See* Climate and social participation
Women, 10, 13. *See also* Gender
  and antiquarianism, 98
  athletic activity and personality traits of, 85
  biological and physical characteristics of, 27
  changing roles of, 21
  increasing participation in sport by, 16
  labor force participation by, 20
  sport and recreational participation by,
    and climatic effects, 10
    and education, 56-57
    and employment, 41-43
    and family size, 49-51
    and marital status, 47-49
    and occupational status, 59, 61
    and opportunity structure, 13

# Y

Youth, 10, 14, 15, 22-23, 27-28, 35, 44, 50, 59, 70, 74-75, 84, 94, 108, 128
  attitudes and participation in sports, 98, 99
  gender differences in, 22, 94